RECOLLECTIONS
OF
THOMAS D. DUNCAN

RECOLLECTIONS
OF
THOMAS D. DUNCAN

A CONFEDERATE SOLDIER

THOMAS D. DUNCAN

Introduction by
JOHN E. TALBOTT, J.D.

BRAYBREE
Publishing

Published by BrayBree Publishing Company LLC
FIRST EDITION

ISBN-13: 978-1-940127-21-7

Printed in the United States of America

BB
BRAY
BREE   BrayBree Publishing Company LLC
P.O. Box 1204
Dickson, Tennessee 37056-1204

Visit our website at www.braybreepublishing.com

DEDICATION

———

THIS brief reminiscent story is affectionately dedicated to my two grandsons, Shelby Curlee, Jr., and William Peyton Dobbins, Jr., in the hope that it may help to teach them two great truths—that the old South that was and is no more, and the gray armies that fought for its glory, its principles, and its institutions, are entitled to their devotion and respect forever; and that the nation by that strife one severed, now reunited and in peace, is inseparable and eternal—the guardian of the highest ideals of mankind, the pioneer of liberty and of world democracy.

THOMAS D. DUNCAN.

CONTENTS

———

Recollections of Thomas D. Duncan

CHAPTER 6
Shiloh 31

CHAPTER 7
Corinth After Shiloh 49

CHAPTER 8
Battle of Rienzi 59

CHAPTER 9
Murfreesboro and Kentucky Campaign 62

CHAPTER 10
The Battle of Corinth 66

CHAPTER 11
West Tennessee 79

CHAPTER 12
Middle Tennessee 83

CHAPTER 13
Pursuit of the Speight Raiders 85

CHAPTER 14
Chickamauga 91

CHAPTER 15
West Tennessee 93

Contents

FOREWORD

———

THIS unpretentious work is not the product of a literary ambition. Though my story deals with events that will live forever in the records of our country, I have not sought to give it the wings of poetic fancy whereby it may fly into the libraries of the earth.

Within the happy family circle, from which my children are now gone, these oft-recounted recollections became a part of their education. I permitted them to turn the pages of my memory, as the leaves of a book, that they might learn the vanished glory of the old South—the loving loyalty and the sad travail of her people. And I trust that they learned also that our unfortunate Civil War—now, thank God, nearly sixty years behind us—was a clash of honest principles.

That there were wild-eyed agitators and extremists on both sides, and that each had its scalawags and low-flung ruffians, there can be no doubt (and some of these—alas!—still live); but the masses of the soldiers of both armies, who bore the brunt of battle and suffered the privations of those sorrowful years, were patriots; and he who speaks or writes to the contrary is an enemy to our reunited country and an element of weakness and danger in the strength of the nation.

My two beloved daughters have prevailed upon me to record my experiences of four years as a Confederate soldier, in the form of a brief printed memoir; and so, impelled by my regard for their wishes, I enter the work for them and for their descendants, without any thought of placing a literary commodity upon the counters of the country; and yet I must so write that, wherever this volume may chance to fall into the hands of a stranger, he may find in it that one essential to such a story as this is—*Truth*.

INTRODUCTION

———

I T has been 155 years since the end of the American Civil War and not quite a century since the publication of Thomas Dudley Duncan's memoir, *Recollections of Thomas D. Duncan, A Confederate Soldier*, in 1922. This little book did not receive a great deal of attention after its initial publication or the next ninety years. I found a copy in 2011 and felt it deserved recognition.

I began carefully reading this little memoir, making annotations and enhancing Duncan's account in places I thought was needed. As I researched the book and the life of its author, Thomas Dudley Duncan, I was concerned that little attention had been paid to the north Mississippi native in Civil War histories and literature. Perhaps his account was not as significant as I believed. Though disheartened, I continued to learn as much as possible about the man and the soldier.

Then in 2012, Thomas Duncan gained new recognition. His memories were featured in the film *Shiloh: Fiery Trial*, which introduces visitors to Shiloh National Military Park. His home in nearby Corinth, Mississippi, was restored. His words were inscribed on the Mississippi state monument erected on the battlefield in 2015.

The work I originally contemplated was an annotated and supplemented edition of Duncan's *Recollections*. Although completed, I decided not to publish it. Frankly, the more I reviewed it, the more it seemed I was distracting from Duncan's account. I did not want that. I want readers in the 21st century to concentrate on his words— *his* emotions and *his* recollections.

I was greatly heartened to see the renewed interest in Duncan. However, the glaring omission in all of this renewed interest has been the lack of his memoir. His life and words have been preserved on film, plaques, and monuments, yet his memoir has been long out of print and not widely available. The publication of this edition is intended to remedy that deficiency.

Duncan's *Recollections* is just what it purports to be—the recollections of a soldier who was decades past the action that molded him into the man he became. It was not meant to be an exhaustive history, but simply one man's memoirs. It is presented here in all of its virtues and limitations with no annotations and no commentary other than this Introduction and the Epilogue hereafter.

With the publication of this edition of *Recollections*, it is the hope of the publishers that it will reach a wider audience who can carry his words with them long after they've visited the battlefields and locations he writes about.

JOHN E. TALBOTT, J.D.
February 22, 2020

ILLUSTRATIONS

Thomas D. Duncan
At the age of fourteen, two years before he rode with
Forrest's famous troop

Thomas D. Duncan
Fifty-seven years after his last ride with Forrest

MRS. JULIETTE ELGIN DUNCAN
Wife of Thomas D. Duncan

xx

A street scene in Corinth, Miss.

The Tishomingo Hotel in Corinth, Miss.

LT. GEN. NATHAN BEDFORD FORREST

FORREST AND HIS MEN ESCAPING FROM FORT DONELSON

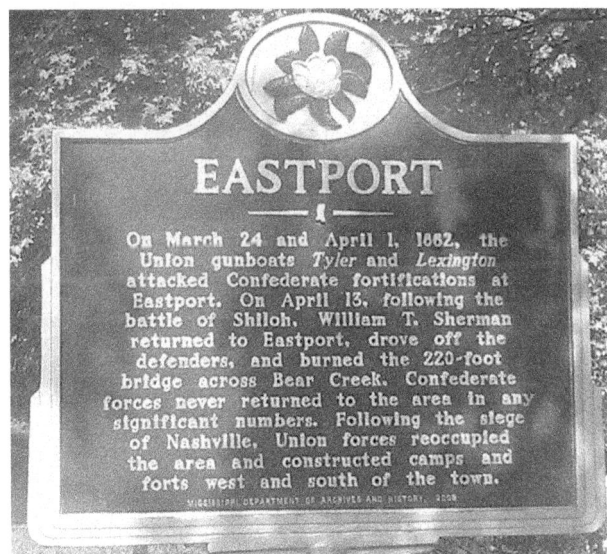

EASTPORT, MISS. HISTORICAL MARKER

Shiloh Church

Federal transports at Pittsburg Landing

"THE NIGHT CAME ON, AND THE CONFEDERATES LAY DOWN IN
LINE OF BATTLE TO REST AND SLUMBER, REALIZING THE DANGER
OF THE COMING MORN AND THE CERTAINTY THAT FOR MANY
THE NEXT SUNRISE WOULD BE THEIR LAST ON EARTH."

THOMAS D. DUNCAN, PVT.
TISHOMINGO RANGERS

MISSISSIPPI MONUMENT AT
SHILOH NATIONAL MILITARY PARK

BATTLE OF CORINTH, MISS. OCT. 4th 1862.

THE BATTLE OF CORINTH

CORINTH, MISS. DURING THE WAR

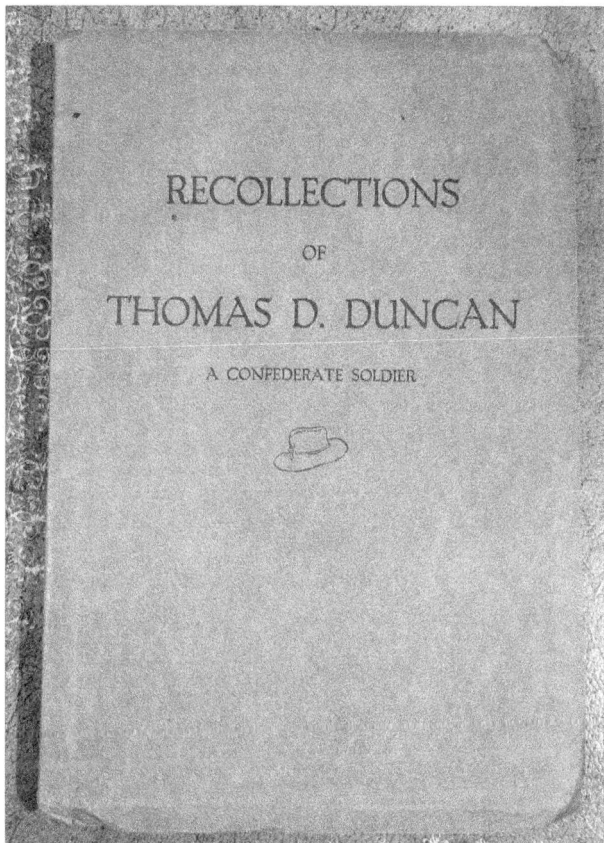

FIRST EDITION COPY OF
RECOLLECTIONS OF THOMAS D. DUNCAN,
A CONFEDERATE SOLDIER

THE DUNCAN HOUSE, CORINTH, MISS.

THOMAS D. DUNCAN TOMBSTONE
HENRY CEMETERY, CORINTH, MISS.

RECOLLECTIONS
OF
THOMAS D. DUNCAN

CHAPTER I

———

THE TOCSIN OF WAR

———

I n yielding to the request which brought forth this effort, I shall not assume the role of the historian nor set myself up as a critic of any command or commander.

Being in my seventy-sixth year, in the calming twilight of life's evening, I feel that I am capable of recording, without prejudice or passion, my impressions of that most heated era of our country, whose momentous events—sad, tragic, glorious—represent the summit of dramatic interest in all my years.

As it is impossible for any two persons to see the same things exactly alike, it is but natural to suppose that I shall present facts at variance with the views of some others; but as my purpose is not that of the controversialist, I shall have no quarrel with any man's views, but to all who may be interested in this narrative I would say that the scenes herein reviewed came within the vision of my eyes, and my highest ambition is to give a truthful reflection from my viewpoint.

I enlisted in the Confederate army, at a very tender age, in April, 1861. My first enrollment was in an infantry company known as the "Corinth Rifles," then being formed and drilled at Corinth, Miss., under the leadership of Judge W.H. Kilpatrick, a worthy and cultured gentleman and a scion of a distinguished Southern family. He was elected captain of the company. The organization was among the first of the Mississippi soldiery and one of the best that enlisted in the cause of the South. But, on account of my youth and rather fragile body, my father objected to my going out with the infantry, and urged me to secure a transfer to a cavalry company that had been organized at Corinth under the guidance of another good Mississippian, the noble-hearted and gallant gentleman, William M. Inge, my older brother being first lieutenant in the company.

My father gave me a good horse, and I was transferred accordingly. Naturally, the first call that came for troops was for infantry and artillery; and the "Corinth Rifles" went to Pensacola, Fla. This was trying indeed to the pride and metal of the young patriots left behind—to see out kin and friends leave for the war. This inner pressure became so strong that a large number of

4

the membership of our cavalry company left our ranks and went with the infantry to Pensacola.

I would have gone, but as I was under the lawful age for enlistment and still subject to parental rule, my father objected; and as the patriotic spirit in me was welling up so strong as to throw out a defy, my father told me that if I did not obey him I should not go to war at all. Such things were different in those days from what they are today. The average boy, however high-spirited, was careful to heed a father's command. Nevertheless, in his kindly solicitude, fearing that I might be persuaded by my comrades to run away, my father earnestly counseled me to remain with the cavalry company, with the understanding that he would offer no objection to my entering the service on account of my age. This settled my obedience to his will, and I was glad to be permitted to be a cavalry soldier.

None knew, except those who lived during those stirring times, the atmosphere of excitement that pervaded this Southern country. Our captain had telegraphed to every possible point to have our company ordered into active service; but no call came, and after the opening gun on Fort Sumter, nothing could longer restrain him, and he left us and went as adjutant, with a Mississippi infantry regiment, to Virginia. This loss came near to disrupting our company, and the ranks to disrupting our company, and the ranks were depleted to twenty troopers. It was discouraging indeed to those who remained.

Here I wish to tell you what was then going on in Corinth and what contributed to holding the nucleus of our company together.

A unit of the first army of Virginia was assembling and organizing at this place, embracing the flower and chivalry of the South—men of culture, wealth, and position mingling with the honest and fearless yeomanry of hills and mountains and valleys; and in most cases it was the first time they had ever spent a night or satisfied a hunger beyond the parental roof or a comfortable home. Indeed, the number in that vast host of the first volunteers who had ever failed to lie down to slumber on an old-fashioned feather bed was small. Few were those who had not known the luxury of the carpeted room or satisfied their appetites from any source except that bountifully laden table so conspicuous in the old Southern home.

It will be remembered by Corinthians of that period who still live that Corinth was dealt a severe and hurtful blow by the soldiers who composed that army. They pronounced it the most unhealthful place on the Western Hemisphere. Evidently they thought it the supreme upas of human ills, overlooking the fact that all was due to the conditions of their camps rather than to any natural causes from water or climate.

From close observation of those camps I was led to believe that under the same conditions the result would have been the same had our men been encamped around the peaks of Ben Vair or on the slopes of the Rockies.

I saw those young, white-handed men, who had never been exposed to a hardship, attempting to cook bread and meat in a frying pan that scorched the outside and left the inside raw. Eating such food and drinking water from surface wells only a few feet deep, into which every rain washed the refuse of the camps, were not diarrhea, typhus, and many other diseases, very natural consequences?

This did insanitation and infection become more deadly enemies than the armed foe, reaping an inglorious harvest of loathsome death among those gallant and fearless boys of the South who had sought to stake their lives beneath a fluttering battle flag.

After a time, this splendid army of the Confederacy was organized and equipped and sent to Virginia. The hurry and bustle of camp life were gone, the ceaseless noises that so long had dinned our ears had died into quietude, and for a period Corinthians were permitted to contemplate, thoughtfully and with misgivings, the war cloud then rapidly approaching.

Meantime the remnant of our cavalry company accepted an invitation to join with a like number from North Alabama, and the consolidated command was ordered to rendezvous at Columbus, Miss., where there were several companies already assembled and forming a regiment of cavalry. We marched through the country, and after four or five days arrived at our destination on a bright, sunny morning. The companies stationed there were lined up along the principle thoroughfares to receive us. In new uniforms and well mounted, these troops seemed the very spirit of war. They were equipped with new and formidable arms, and their horses were in trappings of gay ribbon.

Ordinarily the scene would have been thrilling and inspiring, but the shabby appearance of our company, travel-worn and but few of the men in uniforms or carrying weapons of any kind, presented a contrast that was humiliating and embarrassing. Our general aspect was more that of a bunch of immigrants than of a company of militant patriots. My young heart was almost overcome with shame, for at this stage of the war I was considering the outward appearance rather than the inward condition. I looked upon the great and tragic issue as depending upon tinsel trappings and martial splendor. But in the hard school of experience I was soon to learn a different lesson.

At Columbus we went into camp for instruction, and were taught the use of cavalry arms, how to manage our horses, and were drilled in the tactics and movements of troopers in action. We were also instructed in camp and guard duties and put through the regular service of mounting guard day and night.

I had been in camp only a short while when my time came to go on guard duty. I was detailed to go out on a dark and stormy night. It was a bitter trial for a boy to be out alone in the open, in the blackness of such a night, and to walk up and down a deserted pathway and keep the vigil of the camp. There was no enemy near us, but orders were given and obedience demanded just the same as if a hostile army were in front of us. We were camped along the banks of Luxapeilial, a large creek that flows southeast of Columbus and empties into the waters of the Tombigbee River a short distance south of the city. Etched upon my memory is the trying experience of that first night on guard duty. As I paced my post, the whole camp wrapped in slumber, I thought of home and the comfortable surroundings I had exchanged for this situation. I did not then know much about the "prodigal son," but I have since learned that I was very much in the same condition as he when he came to himself. It was not very cold, but the rain poured down, and there were no other sounds except an occasional neigh of some restless horse and the melancholy hooting of an owl.

My gloomy meditations were suddenly interrupted by the unmistakable sounds of approaching footsteps. We were relieved every three hours; but as the relief guard always had from three to six men, I knew it could not be that. That which I heard seemed to be a solitary being approaching. The orders were that no one should be allowed to pass or come within thirty feet of the guard without a challenge. When challenged, if the intruder could not give the password or countersign, it was the duty of the guard to arrest and hold him until the arrival of the officer with the relief guard.

I had an uncle who served with Jackson in the Seminole War, and he had told me that the first requirement of a good soldier was to obey orders. So when my mysterious visitor came near enough for me to see the outlines of a human form, I said: "Halt! Who goes there?" He answered: "A friend." Whereupon I commanded him to advance ten feet and give the password—if more than one, then one at a time. As there was only one man in sight, he came forward until I halted him again. Then, upon my demand for the password, he said he had forgotten it, but that he was the officer of the guard, and that there would be no impropriety in my permitting him to pass—that he had been permitted to pass the post just beyond me. His story was told with great earnestness; but

I was somewhat out of temper, anyway, standing there in the rain. So I brought my gun to "ready" and told him that he must "mark time"; that he had failed to meet the demands according to orders given me, and that if he attempted to either advance or retire he must take the consequences. Standing only a few feet from an inexperienced boy, excited and frightened, with a cocked gun leveled on him, he realized his danger and quickly called to the relief guard, waiting in the darkness just back of him, to see if he could pass me, and they came forward in proper order and gave the password.

He proved to be a special officer sent out to test the guards on duty. He said to me: "Young man, you have acquitted yourself with great honor in this matter. I have traversed the entire camp to-night, and you are the only sentry who has obeyed his instructions. I have succeeded in deceiving and passing every man on guard except you. In one instance I secured possession of the sentinel's gun; and now I have all of these men here under arrest, and they will have to serve a term in the guardhouse for their neglect of duty. Were we in the presence of the enemy, the penalty for this violation of orders would be death."

This little episode in my first military experience made me the hero of the camp for a time, and I was commended in guard orders in the

highest terms as a boy of fifteen years exhibiting the soldierly qualities of a veteran. Naturally,
my father was very proud of this act and wrote
me a letter abounding in praise.

Thus ends the first chapter of my war story.
Could my military experience have closed with
that preparatory service, I should have saved
the pangs of much sorrow and from out my life
would have been taken the wasting trials and
hardships endured for four long and anxious
years. But – alas – had I been spared the danger
and the suffering, I could never have known the
happy consciousness of duty performed under
the hammer of danger nor tasted the sweet fruit
of satisfaction that grows from the bitter flower
of sacrifice.

CHAPTER 2

———

MOBILIZATION

———

AMID the ever-growing dangers of that anxious year, our little command was ordered to Corinth, where the mobilization of the Western army had begun. To me this was a most welcome move, but for the majority of the boys, who were born and reared in that immediate section, it meant the first breaking of home ties—sad adieus and, to many, the last farewell.

Aside from the partings of kindred, lovers, and friends, there was a poignant sorrow over leaving Columbus, for its air of natural and restful beauty had cast a bewitching charm. Save one, it was the oldest town in Mississippi; and the history of its pioneers, the dim legends of its loves, romances, and tragedies, like its white-columned mansions, were foundationed in the long ago. The hearts of its people, ripe in sentiment and aesthetic culture, had been given in a flood of affectionate gratitude to the young soldiers, training within its gates, to defend the institutions, ideals, and traditions of the South.

Such a town could not but be the nursery of beauty and the home of hospitality, the two most persuasive influences that touch the heart of youth.

Soon after our arrival at Corinth our company was detached from the regiment for special or scout duty. Troops were then being sent to Island No. 10, Columbus (Ky.), Fort Henry, and Fort Donelson, Corinth being a distributing point.

The Confederacy was then establishing a line of defense from Columbus, Ky., on the Mississippi River, to Bowling Green, and on to Cumberland Gap, in Eastern Tennessee; and in the early autumn of 1861 there was much activity along this rather widely spaced line. There had been a slight clash at Columbus, Ky., and the battle of Fishing Creek, on the other end of the line, the most serious consequences of which was the death of the brilliant and promising General Zollicoffer.

The first Bull Run, back in July, had fanned away the last hope of compromise, and both North and South were athrob with the roll of mustering drums.

CHAPTER 3

HENRY AND DONELSON

OUR company left Corinth in September and went through North Alabama and Middle Tennessee, and I joined Forrest and arrived in the vicinity of Nashville in November. After scouting and guarding some convoys down the Cumberland River, we were ordered to support the defenses of Forts Henry and Donelson, on the Tennessee and Cumberland Rivers, respectively, just ten miles apart, where the two rivers parallel each other in their northward courses across Tennessee.

I was now to realize, in my first actual experience, the fullness of the horrors that wait upon the tinsel glory of that long-worshiped art of human destruction which men call "war."

General Forrest had secured, early in the war, several hundred old-styled cap-and-ball navy pistols, most valuable weapons for cavalry.

On December 28, 1861, at Sacramento, Ky., we had our first with a troop of Union cavalry, about equal in number of men to ours. After a sharp engagement, we succeeded in putting the enemy to flight. The Union troopers lost Captain Bacon, killed, and several men killed and wounded, and we lost two men, killed, and several wounded.

After this skirmish, we retired within the lines at Fort Donelson.

On February 6, 1862, General Grant, assisted by the gunboat fleet under Commodore Foote, vigorously attacked and captured Fort Henry, defended by Gen. Lloyd Tilghman.

With the opening of the bombardment, General Grant hurriedly threw his army across the road leading from Fort Henry to Fort Donelson to cut off the possible retreat of Tilghman's command of about three thousand men; but Tilghman, foreseeing the almost certainty of defeat, had kept only enough men to man and handle the guns of the fort and marched his troops in double quick on toward Donelson, just escaping the Union line by a few hundred yards.

This was the first experience under fire of nearly all the soldiers of both sides, and the all-absorbing topic around the camp fires was the exaggerated danger of the gunboats, then a new instrument of war. It was believed by many that they were both indestructible and irresistible;

that, once within range of the enemy, he had no chance of escape; and the soldiers who had been under their fire at Fort Henry gave descriptions of their terror and havoc which did not tend to allay the fears of the uninitiated. We were told that our cannon balls would fall harmless from their steel armor, and that the gunners of these boats were so protected that they could take deliberate aim and deliver their shots into our port holes. In fact, these tales were so enlarged upon that many of our men were paralyzed with fear and became so timid that they did not want to fight when the gunboat was a factor. I shall always believe that this sentiment played a large part in the surrender of Fort Donelson, although when the actual test came at Donelson the Confederate shore batteries outfought the gunboats and gave them a very decisive drubbing; but the one fatal defect in the mechanism of the old-style batteries, which provided no way of depressing the guns to a sufficient angle to bring them in line with a near and lower target, placed our gunners at a great disadvantage here.

I am giving rather liberal space to my comment on this battle, because it was the greatest battle of the war up to that time and because of the supreme confidence of the people, the army and the commanders, in the impregnability of this fort and their consequent disappointment when it fell.

The Confederates successfully repulsed the combined attack of General Grant and Commodore Foote on the first day.

On February 15 another attack was made; and General Forrest, with all the cavalry, and General Pillow, with the infantry and artillery, repelled the land attack, and pushed back the Union Army on the right until this wing was doubled on its center; and if the movement had been given support from the other parts of the Confederate lines, there might have been a different story to tell of Fort Donelson. But it may be that all the "ifs" that have changed the fate of the world belong to the God of battles, who alone knows where to set them in the little affairs of men that they may serve the ultimate good of all his people.

In this engagement Gen. N.B. Forrest displayed, for the first time, that tremendous energy and marvelous generalship which were so prominently and successfully employed in all his future career.

This fight was the most appalling sight I had ever witnessed. I was a mere boy engaged in a struggle wherein men were seeking to destroy each other, and yet I dare say that the common soldiers of those two million hosts had no real and clear conception of the cause of their deadly antagonism.

May the politician and the agitator ponder well this terrible fact and beware of the keen word that may open the veins of a nation!

The sky of my memory must forever hold the shriek of those shells; nor can I forget the muffled crash of grapeshot and minnie balls as they literally tore the ranks of the combatants.

At one point in our advance we were ordered to charge a battery of field guns. In this charge I lost control of my horse, and he carried me beyond the battery into the infantry support of the enemy. I made a circuit, and on my return a Federal soldier fired at me when I was not more than twenty paces from him. I was mounted on a spirited animal, and it was running and jumping so unevenly that I happily made a very evasive target, and the soldier missed his aim, just grazing my right shoulder, taking the width of the ball out of my coat and cutting a crease in the flesh. The shot was fired as I was approaching the man; and as I passed within a few feet of him, I shot at him twice with my six-shooter, but could not tell whether or not my shots struck him. I was a good marksman, and under ordinary circumstances I would have been sure of my aim; but it behooves me to tell you that I was far more bent on getting out of this dangerous situation than on killing an enemy.

I had many narrow escapes that day, but this was my closest "call" as a soldier of the C.S.A.

On our part of the field our forces had been successful, but the remainder of our lines had been defeated, and the fort had been so battered that those in command—Generals Floyd, Buckner, and Pillow—decided to surrender on the following morning.

General Forrest was advised of the plan, and he informed the commanders that he did not become a soldier to surrender and that he was going out that night and take as many of his men as would follow him. The backwater was from two to six feet deep, but this had no terror for our leader. We secured the service of a native to guide us, and by going in close to the Union line we found shallow water and no obstruction, and so we escaped to safety. The ground was covered with snow and the water was very cold.

Forrest led his troops to safety on this occasion under conditions which would have broken the will of any ordinary man, as he was to do many times in the years that followed.

CHAPTER 4

CORINTH AGAIN THE CENTER

WITH the fall of Donelson, the Confederate line was broken at the center; and Gen. Albert Sidney Johnston, then in command of all the Confederate forces of Tennessee and Kentucky, evacuated Columbus and Bowling Green and withdrew his army to the Memphis and Charleston Railroad, establishing a new line of defense, with Tennessee and Kentucky, thus early in the struggle, practically in the hands of the enemy.

Through Tennessee, North Alabama, and North Mississippi I returned to Corinth, which place had become the headquarters of General Johnston.

The capture of Henry and Donelson constituted a severe blow to the Confederacy. A vast, rich territory and a splendid army had been lost, and the Tennessee and Cumberland Rivers opened to the Union forces.

To hold the line of the Southwestern defense, already pushed back to the very margin of the great Mississippi Valley, and to protect the railroad of communication and transportation between the East and the West (the Memphis and Charleston), General Johnston began mobilization at Corinth, with the purpose not only to defend, but to counter attack as soon as possible. It developed early in March that the Union forces were seeking an outlet up the Tennessee to some point from which the new Confederate line could be attacked.

With a few companies I was sent to Eastport, then the head of navigation on the Tennessee River, to scout and watch for the expected landing of the Union army. Soon came the gunboats Lexington and Tyler, invested with a silent terror, wrought by superstitious fear, more awful than their guns. It was only with a closer knowledge that this unwarranted fear vanished. Later in the war we captured one of these monsters at this point with loaded battery, and still later Forrest captured three gunboats and ran a flotilla of this class off the river with Morton's and Rice's field batteries.

At this time there lived at Eastport a man named Hill who had been a steamboat pilot, and he had a son just about my age; so by arrangement I dressed in one of the suits of his son and went with Mr. Hill to the landing. As we were the only persons present, three officers came ashore and asked Hill many questions about the Southern soldiers. They did not notice me on account of my age and unsophisticated dress; but I was using my eyes for all they were worth, and afterwards, with Mr. Hill's assistance, I was able to give a fairly good description of the floating terrors. They were old wooden transports armored with railroad irons and with small iron above the water line and pilot house.

After this episode, the force at Iuka sent a battery of field pieces to Chickasaw Bluff, just above Eastport, from which position they had a clear view down the river to the first bend, about four miles.

The commander made up a detail from our company to keep watch at Eastport for the next appearance of the gunboats. On the riverbank was an old elevator topped with a tower by which grain and produce could be loaded and unloaded into steamboats. We used this old building as a watch tower at night, and during the day we were stationed on the high bluff, two of us watching together. One night my companion and I had been discussing the probability of being able to discern the approach of a gunboat, as they concealed all lights and muffled the exhaust of their engines. In the darkness and the silence our conversation turned to idle fancies. To the soldier actually engaged in war death seems ever near, and, with the mind so attuned, it is but a step from the natural to the supernatural. My companion has asked me if I believed in ghosts, or in the appearance on earth of the spirits of the dead. I told him that from spirits of the dead. I told him that from the old slaves of my father I had imbibed the superstitious fear of ghosts, or, as they called them, "hants;" but that as I had grown older, my mind had been disabused of the hair-raising philosophy of headless men and white-sheeted women. "Then," said he, "I will tell you a story of this place."

As a solemn and somewhat uncanny prelude to his story, he slowly repeated the couplet,

"Into the sea, out of the sea,
All that is mine comes back to me;"

and continued: "In the year 1845 a steamboat captain named Moore was running on the Tennessee between Eastport, Miss., and Paducah, Ky. His wife had been lost in a river disaster; but he had a daughter, beautiful and accomplished, whose rearing had been the pressing care of his lonely life. After her school days, the young lady spent much of her time on her father's boat and with friends here at Eastport. The pride of her father's heart and with many admirers, she was 'the observed of all observers' at all the balls and other social functions so frequent on the boat which was the center of life for this lonely section. It soon developed, as is nearly always the case, that the young man who won her heart was not her father's choice among her many suitors.

"When the young lovers could not reconcile the father to their promised marriage, they stole away from the boat on a dark night when the river was at high stage, climbed to the top of this old tower, lashed themselves together, and jumped into the raging waters; and it is said that to this day, when the river runs high and the moon is gone and the clouds curtain the stars, the spirits of those long-gone lovers return to the base of this tower and struggle again with the engulfing waves, and wild sounds rise from the rushing waters as if a man had moaned and a woman shrieked."

As he finished his blood-curdling story, there was an unearthly scream in the loft above us, and we executed a retreat out of that old building, which for prompt action and swift movement would have commanded the admiration of Napoleon or Stonewall Jackson, even though our courage as soldiers had gone to pieces upon the phantom of superstition.

We had disturbed the slumber or meditation of a screech owl, and with one shrill whistle he had hustled us from our post of duty more hastily than could have been done by all the "Yankee" gunboats on the river.

CHAPTER 5

———

STRANGE OUTCOME
OF A FALSE ALARM

———

AFTER deserting the old warehouse as our picket post, we had to make some kind of "frame up" to report to our captain of the guard. It was about one mile to where the reserve was encamped on the hill. We mounted our horses and went up, very much excited from the owl scare, and told the officer that we are sure that we had heard a boat approaching; and instantly the camp became a center of activity. The battery at Chickasaw Bluff was notified to be ready for action at daylight, and a runner was sent to Iuka to notify the commander that the gunboats were approaching and with orders to be in readiness to send a sufficient force to prevent a landing upon call.

As I witnessed all this commotion and preparation based upon our falsehood, my conscience smote me bitterly, and I do not know what would have become of us but for the fact that the gunboats actually came. While all except the two false messengers waited in expectancy, soon after daylight, two boats came into view, approaching cautiously. When opposite the landing, they stopped for a little while and then turned to go back down the river. It was then that the battery at Chickasaw Bluff opened fire on them. Our gunners were poor marksmen and could not make a hit; so, after the exchange of a few shots, the boats dropped down the river.

Two years later Morton's battery of our command, from this same point literally riddled and captured a gunboat of this type.

It was apparent that the purpose of the enemy was to land a force as near the railroad as possible, and Eastport seemed the natural point, as Iuka, on the railroad, was only eight miles away; but the discovery that Eastport was in the hands of the Confederates and the fact that the surrounding hills and bluffs were peculiarly adapted to defense probably caused the Federal commander to change his plan.

After the gunboats had sailed away, I was selected, with three comrades, to follow down the river bank and watch for the chosen landing place of the Union Army. When crossing Yellow Creek just above where it flows into the river, there was a gunboat shelling the woods. Leaving the river where it makes a bend, we rode across the neck of land to Childer's Hill,

in front of Hamburg. We could see the smoke of
a steamer that seemed to be lying at the wharf;
and as we expected troops to land here, we were
discussing the advisability of going down to
the village, when the boat fired a solid shot at
us, which passed over our heads. We immediately whirled our horses into the woods, bearing down the river, when the second shot came
and hit the ground we had just left. We went on
down toward Pittsburg Landing, and the gunboats shelled the woods along the river between
Hamburg and Pittsburg Landing during all of
the afternoon.

About dark we arrived at the home of Thomas Fraley, near Shiloh Church, and accepted his
invitation to spend the night under his roof. He
told us that he had visited the Landing late in
the afternoon, and that no troops were there,
but that the gunboats were very active between
this place and Hamburg, where, he was sure,
troops were being landed; that two transports of
soldiers had passed up the river during the day,
probably to be landed at Hamburg or at some
place above there. We did not then know, what
developed later, that the Federal commander,
after abandoning Eastport as a landing place,
had selected the mouth of Yellow Creek, above
Hamburg. But it was impossible to get a foot-
ing there, as the water was all over the landing
place. So the transports dropped back to Pitts-

burg Landing, which place was finally selected from sheer necessity on account of its high
bluff and its ridge road leading from the river to
Corinth, Miss., twenty-two miles away.

Apprehending no danger in spending the
night with our friend, Fraley, though very close
to the river, we turned in for the night, enjoying
a good supper and a comfortable bed. This home
was a short distance west of Shiloh Church, on
the Stantonville Road.

Rain was falling the next morning, and so
we did not hurry away. Thus early in the war
soldiers were guilty of many things which a year
later would not have been tolerated. After the
sections had grappled each other in the deadly
conflict, there was no more sleeping in houses
within gunshot of the enemy without a picket
or vidette.

About eight o'clock, while we were saddling
our horses, some country boys passed, riding
mules, and told us they were going down to the
Landing. In a few minutes we bade adieu to our
friend, Fraley, and, after riding down the road
a short distance, we turned into the woods to
strike the country road leading back to Hamburg. When we crossed the Corinth and Pittsburg Landing Road, we discovered a regiment
of cavalry passing in the direction of Pea Ridge,
and we soon became aware of the presence of
large bodies of troops being disembarked at

Pittsburg Landing. Fully appreciating our danger, we avoided all roads and went to Corinth and apprised General Johnston of the landing place of the Federal Army.

Shortly after this I saw Mr. Fraley, and he told me how narrowly I had escaped being captured. As we were leaving his house, a regiment of cavalry came up at a gallop, four absent, with guns ready for action. We had just turned a bend in the road, which hid us from view. The colonel of the regiment asked Mr. Fraley what had become of the soldiers who were there a few minutes ago. He told them we had just left, and they rode rapidly down the road after us. So it happened that our turning into the woods was all that saved us.

I have related this incident somewhat at length to illustrate the necessity of unbroken vigilance and the danger of the slightest carelessness in time of war.

The Federal transports had begun disembarking troops that morning, and, very naturally, they advanced along the roads leading away from the Landing, taking possession of the country for several miles west of the river.

As soon as General Johnston learned of this latest move of the enemy he began his arrangements to meet it.

CHAPTER 6

SHILOH

HERE has been so much written about the battle of Shiloh that it is not in order for me to seek to contradict or confirm any of the various claims and theories. I shall adhere to my determination to make this story a record of scenes and events actually observed. I was in the battle of Shiloh from the opening gun to the close; and while I was very young, the impressions made on my mind are vivid and lasting. Notwithstanding the flight of sixty years, I remember many circumstances of that terrible conflict, as if they had happened yesterday.

As soon as General Johnston assumed command of the new line centered at Corinth, he began mobilization on the largest possible scale; and on March 29, 1862, he issued an order consolidating the armies of Kentucky and Mississippi and all independent commands into "The Army of the Mississippi," naming Gen. G.T.

Beauregard as second in command and Gen. Braxton Bragg as chief of staff. Gen. Van Dorn, stationed at Little Rock, Ark., had been ordered to report with his army at Corinth; but for some reason he did not reach there in time to participate in the battle of Shiloh.

It was reported to us that, following the battle of Fort Donelson, General Halleck, the commander of the Department of the Mississippi, and General Grant, acting under him, were not in harmony, and that Halleck has suspended Grant and placed Gen. C.F. Smith in active command of the army, and that he had established camps at Pittsburgh Landing preparatory to the expected movement against Johnston's line.

It came to light later that, a few days prior to the battle of Shiloh, General Smith, in stepping into a launch from a steamboat, had sprained his ankle and was disabled, which resulted in General Grant being again placed in command.

It was a current report that General Smith, after being disabled, had gone on a visit to General Halleck at St. Louis, and that General Sherman had been left in temporary command of the encampment at Pittsburg Landing.

When the battle opened, General Grant was at the W.H. Cherry residence, at Savannah, Tenn., eight miles from the battlefield.

General Johnston had been informed that Buell's army was marching from Middle Tennessee to join Grant's army at Pittsburgh Landing, thus giving the Union force a numerical superiority of approximately thirty thousand men; and as it was not possible for Van Dorn to reach Corinth before the arrival of Buell, General Johnston decided to make a surprise attack on the encampment at Pittsburgh Landing. Hence, on April 1, we began preparation for a forward movement.

I was detailed as a courier at Beauregard's headquarters; and as I knew the country around Corinth, I had been used in many cases in piloting the incoming troops to the encampment and in carrying messages between the different commanders. In this way I became acquainted with the contemplated movement of our army. I was not aware of the destination but could see the feverish preparation for a move of some kind. It was General Johnston's plan to have all of his troops before the Federal Army on the 4th of April and to fight the battle on the 5th; but the bad condition of the roads, resulting from long-continued rains, so delayed the progress of the troops that the hindmost corps did not get into position until about dark on the evening of April 5.

General Johnston had instructed his commanders to guard the secret of our approach.

Late in the afternoon of the 5th, while we were waiting for the final touches of the attacking formation, I rode out to a high point in front of our center, and I could hear the Union troops drilling in their encampment. The drum and fife and the commands of the officers could be plainly heard.

It will be remembered that certain Federal commanders always claimed that their troops were not surprised at Shiloh, but I shall always believe that the Union Army was absolutely unaware of the presence of the Confederate Army. They knew that there was a cavalry force in their front, as we had had skirmishes with them, participated in by small detachments on each side.

As I look back over the past, I cannot but believe that Fate had decreed that the Southern Confederacy should fail. We had lost Forts Henry and Donelson, with more than fifteen thousand picked men. Now we were preparing for the greatest pitched battle of the war, and apparently had all the advantage, and yet from an almost insignificant cause we were robbed of the fruits of complete victory.

Advancing from my position on the hill, I rode down to the Corinth Road. Our cavalry had just pushed back a squad of Federal cavalry that had come out toward our line, and this troop soon returned with a larger body of men;

but as we were endeavoring to avoid an engagement, we fell back a little on our reserve. This only encouraged the "Yankees," and in their eagerness to capture us they chased us through our infantry line on the main road, which permitted them to pass through without firing on them on account of the order not to disclose our presence. But this troop kept up the chase until they came upon one of our batteries in the road, and this battery fired on them with two guns, killing some of them and throwing the entire body into confusion; whereupon we turned and followed them back to their line, capturing several men and an officer. When we took them through our line and they saw the situation, the officer exclaimed: "My Lord, our people do not suspect such a thing as this!"

All of this happened just at dark on the evening of the 5th; and, of course, all of our comrades believed that the firing of the cannon would arouse the whole Union Army and reveal the presence of our force.

The night came on, and the Confederates lay down in line of battle to rest and slumber, realizing the danger of the coming morn and the certainty that for many the next sunrise would be the last of earth.

The 6th was Sunday, and the sun came up bright and unclouded. At daybreak I carried a message to Colonel Gilmer, Bragg's chief of artillery, and then rode out to the skirmish line. Here I saw, for the first time, a soldier killed. All the men of the skirmish line were behind trees, and were shooting at such an angle as to enfilade the enemy's position.

The soldier whose killing I witnessed was a Confederate—a very young man. The bullet came from a point several degrees to the right of his front and cut his throat.

Seeing this boy killed impressed me anew with the horrors of war. I thought of his mother, probably praying for him in her distant home, and yet within a few hours his body would be cast into an isolated and unmarked grave.

My musings were suddenly interrupted by a soldier exclaiming, "Look!" and as I cast my eyes in the direction indicated, I saw a long line of bayonets rising over the top of a hill about six hundred yards distant. This force was a brigade of infantry; and as they reached the top of the elevation, our skirmish line fired on them from their hidden position behind trees. The enemy could not see them; and as our company of cavalry was in plain view, they fired at us across the corner of the "Fraley field." We did not have a man hit, but they got several of our horses. A bullet struck the handle of my saber. Another cut a twig from a bush within a few inches of my face, and a flying splinter struck me just above my left eye, and naturally I thought it was a bullet. The pain was so severe and I was so blind that I felt sure that the eye had been destroyed; but a comrade, after examining the wound, assured me that it was only a scratch.

As our company was an escort to a general officer, our commander would not permit us to return the fire, but turned and moved us briskly over the hill out of view of the enemy.

Our presence here, so far in front of our battle line, was due to the fact that General Bragg had sent us with Gilmer, his chief of artillery, to select a route for the guns, as he had to bring them into action through a dense growth of timber. Soon after we had left the hill where the enemy had fired on us we met the Confederate line of battle going into action. This was the grandest, most solemn and tragic scene I had ever witnessed. The sun was just coming up over the hilltop, its bright rays touching the half-green forest with a golden beauty that could not but charm the eye and thrill the heart even in the presence of death. It was one of those rare mornings that, in a deep woods, casts a charm of mingled silence and wild music. In this sunlit antechamber of carnage there were bird songs and the tongueless voices of whispering waters—timid, blended melodies of uncounted centuries that here had sounded their glad chorus to all the mornings of the springtime since trees first grew and rains first fell, since mosses first floored the virgin valets and primal grasses climbed the fresh slopes of the new-born hills.

The intermittent firing had ceased, and the restful music of nature was broken only by the tramp of men and horses. Youth, young manhood, and the middle-aged were mixed in these advancing columns of the South's best blood, and the unspoken thought upon every face was that many were marching to certain death.

This line, the first in the Confederate advance, unrolled as it moved until it reached a maximum length of nearly three miles, covering the entire approach to the Federal Army. The unevenness of the ground and other natural obstacles sometimes broke the continuity of the line, but the gap was soon closed as the militant host swung forward.

Under the ordinary conditions of camp life and of the field of the preparatory drill, the good-natured rivalry of cavalry and infantry would show at every opportunity. The infantry would jeer the cavalry as "buttermilk rangers," and the dragoons would retaliate with "web-footed beef eaters." But on this morning of their first baptism of fire it was different. There was no word spoken, and on every face was pictured solemn and anxious thought. None but God could know how many would emerge safely from that valley of death into which they were about to descend.

When the Confederate line encountered the Union Army, it seemed to me that the two lines fired at the same time, and one excitable soldier in our command exclaimed: "Boys, the war is over! Every man is killed on both sides!" He had been a squirrel hunter, and had never heard anything like a volley of musketry. After the first volley, the roar of guns was continuous throughout the day.

General Sherman, who was in our immediate front, was a veteran of the Mexican War, and he had hurriedly posted his men on an elevation that was covered with a thick growth of timber and underbrush, which almost entirely concealed his line. While our line was in motion, we had to approach up a considerable rise to reach the top of the ridge. The enemy could deliver his fire at us while lying flat on the ground, but our line was compelled to fire while moving. The object of the Confederate commander was to move his army quickly into close range, as the Union Army was equipped with greatly superior arms.

Our men were armed with the old-style, smooth-bored muskets that would not carry over one hundred yards with any degree of accuracy, and we could not afford to stop and try to shoot it out with an adversary armed with long-ranged rifles. Besides, the enemy was surprised by the sudden attack, and we had much to gain from their immediate unpreparedness by pressing for closer action. The Union commander was unable to bring all his men to the rescue; and if we could keep his front rank pressed and falling back, it would be sure to demoralize the rear formation.

General Forrest once said that he would rather have a "five-minutes bulge than a week of tactics," and I think that much of his great success was due to the application of this theory.

I have more than once viewed the sickening wreck of battle, the devastation of cyclones, and the havoc of railroad accidents, and wondered how any human being could pass through such mills of destruction unharmed. On this occasion, as on many others, I saw men go through a veritable hail of lead and iron unscathed, and I had the feeling that is was the providence of God.

Thus far the Confederate line at some points had met with resistance, but the fighting advance was steady until the Union forward camp had been penetrated and both wings had been turned on the center.

When I rode through the first camp, the kettles on the fires were steaming with boiling water, and meat and bread were cooking in the ovens; but the enemy had to go hungry that day. I saw the bodies of a few Union soldiers who had been killed in their tents and horses shot down at the hitching posts in the rear of the camps.

A large rubberized blanket was my part of the spoils that came with the early surprise, and this trophy afterwards proved very serviceable. In all my service of four years I never saw a battle field as rich in the legitimate spoils of war as was the field of Shiloh.

As a courier, I had opportunities far above the average soldier to observe the wreck of battle, and I think the greatest number of killed and wounded lay in the narrow valley of the Shiloh Spring Branch on both sides of the Corinth and Pittsburg Landing Road. The ground was literally covered with dead and dying men.

In passing this point, my horse received a bullet in one of his front legs, and I was compelled to secure a new mount.

Near this place General Bragg had a horse killed under him, and another near the Landing later in the day.

Soon after passing this center of carnage I witnessed a singular thing. A grapeshot, striking the limb of a tree under which a number of mounted officers had gathered, glanced downward and struck a horse just in the rear of the saddle, penetrating his body and entering the ground. The horse was killed instantly, but the rider was not injured.

At this time the outlook was bright for the Confederate arms. About the middle of the day, the Union Army, in falling back and taking new positions, lodged the commands of Prentiss and W.H.L. Wallace in a thick woods, which after the fight was called the "Hornet's Nest," and this place proved a great surprise for both defendants and assailants. Through it runs an old, deserted highway, now known in history as the "Sunken Road." Worn by the travel and flushed by the rains and snows of many years, this remote and unpretentious road became a most welcome trench of protection to the troops of Prentiss and Wallace. Between this road and the approaching Confederate lines was a thick woods, which completely cut off the view of the attacking regiments and forced them to move against an unseen foe.

And so this long-hidden and almost forgotten road, with its fringe of greening woods, proved a pitfall of death and disaster to the Confederate Army and, in my opinion, the salvation of the Union Army.

Soon after the attack on this position began Gen. A.S. Johnston was killed, and, of course, this had a disconcerting effect on the Confederates. To lose the supreme head of an army in such a crisis, however able may be his successor, is to approach the brink of defeat, for an event so dramatic and mournful cannot but shock the very heart of an advancing army and throw it into a temporary paralysis. Such was the condition of the Confederate host at Shiloh at 2:30 P.M. on April 6, 1862.

As soon as General Beauregard was apprised of General Johnston's death, he gathered his bleeding forces and hurled regiment after regiment against the "Hornet's Nest," with its "sunken road" of destiny, sweeping all supporting artillery of the enemy from that portion of the field; but the gray troops could not see the hidden line of blue until they were within a few feet of the old road. The Union troops would suddenly rise out of the ground, fire, and sink from view again.

Only after a long and concentrated fire from sixty-two pieces of Confederate artillery under General Ruggles did the blue line of the "sunken road" abandon its fateful trench of chance and fall back. Then both of its flanks were turned. General Wallace was mortally wounded, and General Prentiss, with more than two thousand troops, was captured. But—alas!—the hours wasted before that "sunken road" brought us in weariness too near the edge of the approaching night; and, with a seeming victory in our grasp, with the brave, though depleted and disorganized army of blue at bay at the ricer's brink, we saw the battle cease for that day; and in the early falling shadows and through the long, long night came the troops of Lew Wallace and of Buell, unscathed and fresh, and twenty-five thousand strong.

This was a sad development to our tired army that had fought without ceasing for eleven hours; and at about 6 o'clock we were withdrawn to the Union camps, where we fell into the obliterating sleep of exhaustion. I was lying on my rubber blanket, and about midnight there was such a downpour of rain as I have seldom seen. My blanket held water so well that I was partly submerged when I woke, and the remainder of the night was spent in cat naps, sitting on the ground with my back against a tree.

On Monday morning, the 7th, the battle opened with not less than twenty-five thousand fresh troops added to Grant's sorely pressed lines, and so the Confederate hopes of Shiloh took wings; but in the deep gloom of the changed situation, our army went into battle line with the coming of the day. Every Confederate had heard the disheartening news; but they were soldiers still, and, with a courage that at this far-distant day is difficult to understand, they held the enemy to a very slow advance until past the hour of noon.

With no Confederate reënforcements in prospect, General Beauregard began, early in the afternoon, to withdraw the gray army from the unequal conflict. We retired in good order and were deeply surprised that the Union forces made no attempt to pursue us beyond their encampment.

We marched back to Corinth, taking with us all captured cannon and other arms, without a rear-guard fight.

General Forrest stopped at the village of Pea Ridge, about eight miles from the battlefield, and on Tuesday, with all the cavalry he could get together, met a division of the enemy which had advanced to Monterey. As we charged this column, General Forrest's horse became unmanageable and carried him through and beyond the Union line, and we felt sure that he would be either killed or captured; but, after turning his horse, he charged back through a troop of the enemy and miraculously escaped with a wound in the foot.

Thus ended the battle of Shiloh, the first grand battle of the great war.

It is almost inconceivable that a battle so great and so deadly was fought by men unacquainted with the harrowing art of war—raw troops thrown hastily together, a citizen soldiery that had never marched to battle except through the pages of books, white-handed Robin Hoods of the orchard and the meadow—indeed, "boys" in years as well as in that glorious comradeship of danger and death; and yet the "Old Guard" of Napoleon never "fixed bayonets" with firmer courage than that which made history on the field of Shiloh sixty years ago.

The soldiers of Johnston's army were armed with a variety of guns which looked more like the gathered heirlooms of a museum than arms of battle—shotguns, squirrel rifles, antiquated muskets, and a few modern rifles.

The Union troops, for the most part, were neither so new to war no so poorly armed as the Confederates, many of them having been in the fights of Henry and Donelson, and the entire army being equipped with the latest improved firearms.

But, considering all things, history must march these two armies of blue and gray down the years, bannered with a fadeless glory; and the great National Park which the government has established on their battle field is a beautiful and impartial testimonial which will speak to the centuries.

To the friends and schoolmates of my youth who were among the killed of this great struggle, my heart has paid sixty years of silent tribute. My last glimpses of some of them, as the smoke of the conflict wrapped them in its thundering folds, have become vivid and cherished memories. It is the strange way of nature that the vanished spirits of my comrades linger in my vision as boys in the joyous flush of life's morning, while I have marched far up into the gray hills of the evening twilight, and I salute them across the long stretch of years.

I had, as I thought, many narrow escapes from death at Shiloh. At one time a cannon ball passed so near me that the current of air created by its passage almost swept me from my horse. Many bullets and grapeshot fanned me and left their unwelcome whistle in my memory.

Amid all the dangers of battle ever walks the spirit of humor, and there is no day so terrible that it fails to hold some laughable incident. I recall one such on the Shiloh field which illustrates the fact that man is the wildest creature of the animal kingdom when thoroughly frightened. Early on Monday morning a small squad of us was preparing a hasty breakfast of "hardtack" and bacon behind our line, having staked our horses out to bushes, when firing began suddenly on the line, followed by the passage of a wild-eyed rider, proclaiming the arrival of Buell at Hamburg, shouting that he was surrounding us and warning us to run for our lives. There was a large, long-haired trooper in our crowd, who made a hurried run for his horse, mounted him, and put the spurs to him, overlooking the fact that the horse was tied to a bush with a long rope. As the spurs went home in the horse's flanks, he began wildly racing around the bush, taking as wide a circle as his line would allow. The excited trooper tossed his head from side to side, trying to keep an eye on the firing line, while the horse increased his speed and narrowed his circle as the rope gradually wound around the bush until it became so tight that it brought him to a sudden stop and sent the trooper on a flying dive to the ground. We were all laughing at him when he ended his wild race, and he was so embarrassed and humiliated that he secured a transfer to another company.

Immediately after our return to Corinth I was detailed to pilot the corps of engineers in locating the line of breastworks that was to protect our front against the advance of the Union Army from Shiloh battlefield.

CHAPTER 7

———

CORINTH AFTER SHILOH

———

C APTAIN J.H. Lockett was chief of the corps of engineers in throwing the line of fortifications around Corinth.

We made the first general survey, commencing at a point on the Memphis and Charleston (now the Southern) Railway about one mile and a half east of Corinth and running north and west in a circle, keeping about the same distance from the town until we came to the Ijams crossing, west of Corinth.

I felt keenly the responsibility of my work as a pilot, but in boyhood and youth I had learned the faces of these hills and woods as one comes to know the kindly countenances of loving friends. In these quite places I had played every game known to the boys of my day, including "Hookey." I knew where the landscape smiled with sunny meadows or laughed with purling springs or frowned with the gloom of a tangled thicket or grew calm and dignified in the cooling shadows of stately groves.

Just how well we did our work was never put to a test, as our army withdrew from Corinth before it was assailed; but our knowledge of the country and of the necessities of that troubled time is mutely reflected in the remaining sections of that great coil of clay, in its segment of seven miles, still plainly visible after the rains and snows and frosts and freezes have charged against them through sixty years.

At the point in our line of fortifications where the road forks, one prong going eastward by Box Chapel and Farmington and the other in a northeasterly direction to Pea Ridge and Pittsburg Landing, we built double communicating lines and placed siege guns.

When we had finished our fortifications and mounted heavy guns at the points of greatest danger, we settled down to await the approach of the Union Army under the direct command of General Halleck, moving upon us with an extreme and timid caution, which forever consigned him to a place among the world's smallest commanders of great armies.

One cannot imagine Lee or Grant or Stonewall Jackson or W.T. Sherman taking more than a month to cover twenty miles in pursuit of a smaller and defeated army. Napoleon or Hannibal, at Shiloh on the night of April 7, 1862, would have found the Confederate Army or the gates of Corinth before sunrise the next morning.

Heretofore in our fights in this theater of war the Union forces had enjoyed the cooperation of the gunboats, and now we were all elated over the prospect of meeting the enemy out of range of his floating batteries.

I was too young to know anything of the strategy of war, but the knowing ones were pointing out the reasons why the Confederates had to defend Corinth. It was as the crossing of the only two trunk lines in the South at that time, and by these lines the Confederacy could transport whatever supplies, men, and guns it possessed to this point. Corinth was the key to the richness of the Mississippi Valley and the outer gateway to the Eastern South; and so if with these reasons urging Richmond, Corinth and these two essential lines of transportation could not be saved, the future of the Confederacy would be dark indeed. My father made this gloomy forecast to me when Corinth was evacuated; and although I fought on as a stern duty, I never again hoped for the success of our cause.

About the first of May, General Beauregard, desiring information regarding the movements of the enemy, called on the detail for three reliable scouts who knew the country and were willing to undertake a dangerous expedition within the Union lines, saying that he did not wish us to go as spies, but as Confederate soldiers, in full uniform, armed, and well mounted, notwithstanding the fact that it would be necessary for us to keep out of sight as much as possible. Dr. Lowry and Mose Austin responded to the call, and insisted that I should be the third man, as I knew the country and could guide them. Setting out early one morning, we traveled the main road until we passed our advanced pickets, and then took to the woods, moving cautiously and in single file until we were well within the Union lines.

About two and a half miles beyond Chambers' Creek we came to the southwest corner of an old, abandoned plantation—no signs of its vanished life except an old house in a state of decay. There being no evidence of human occupants, we decided to rest our horses and investigate the house and the country beyond. Riding forward in single file across the opening between the woods and the house, Austin in front, Lowry next, and I in the rear, when within fifty feet of the front door, six Union soldiers stepped out from behind the house, covered us with their guns, and commanded us to halt. This we had already done. In the tense moment I remembered the quickness and speed of my horse. I knew that Lowry would not surrender, and neither did I intend to. When one of the men commanded us to come forward one at a time, Austin rode forward. This put him directly between us and the firing squad, and I took the opportunity and gave my horse a quick turn and told him to go. He wheeled so quickly that I came near losing my balance and falling, but I lay down and put my arms around his neck and did not try to check his speed until I had received the fire of the squad. Dr. Lowry used the same tactics, and he afterwards told me that he had thought out the same plan, but feared that I would not do as I did do and that our horses would get in a mix-up and cause us to be killed or captured.

Our enemy, having muzzle-loading guns, had no time to reload before we were out of range.

I have always considered this one of my narrowest escapes from death.

We knew that we had no time to lose, as the Federal cavalry would soon be informed as to our presence; so we diverted our course from the route we had come, traveling westward toward the Memphis and Charleston Railroad, and escaped without further contact with the enemy.

We never again saw our comrade, Mose Austin. He was sent to Cairo, Ill., and died in prison.

About two weeks after this episode I was sent with a message to General Price's headquarters at the old Bogle Place, beyond the Stevenson Hill. It developed that the message contained information relative to the advance of the Union Army, then approaching Old Farmington, on the Hamburg and Farmington Road.

When I delivered the message, I was informed that it was desired that the information be repeated to the colonel in command of the picket east of Seven-Mile Creek, and, with this order, I set out upon my prolonged mission. As I had to pass through Old Farmington, where our company was encamped, I stopped long enough to persuade Bailey Donnelly to accompany me. Leaving the main road, we took a cattle trail along Seven-Mile Creek, thence across a swamp, to the east of which we found a country of thick undergrowth. Keeping in this for some distance, we struck the road again, and I soon delivered my message. We hastened to return; and just as we were ready to leave the road for the country of thick undergrowth, we discovered a lone horseman coming over the top of the ridge above us. Slipping into the thicket, we dismounted, tied our horses, and cautiously crept back to ascertain whether the traveler was friend or foe. We soon discovered that he was deeply distressed and in a state of bewilderment. Riding first in one direction and then in another, he seemed to become more and more excited and confused. I was much excited when he came close enough for us to see that he wore the uniform of a Union officer. He finally turned down toward us; and when he was close to us, we steeped from out hiding place and commanded him to surrender. He obeyed without any show of resistance, exhibiting great surprise and excitement, as he, at first, took us for guerillas ready to kill him. We explained to him that we were regular soldiers, and that his ultimate misfortune would be to become a prisoner. After disarming him, we mounted him on his own horse and took him to our command at Farmington. I took his six-shooters, and Donnelly his saddle and his sword, turning in his horse to the army with the prisoner.

He told us that he was Major Phillips, of some Illinois regiment, and that he was reconnoitering in front of his line and became separated from his regiment and lost his way.

Since the war I have endeavored to locate Major Phillips, but have never heard of him. I think he was sent from Corinth to prison at Demopolis, Ala. If still living, I am sure that he would feel some interest in meeting one of his captors of that lone-gone time of stress and danger and sorrow.

In a few days after my return, General Pope threw a division of the Union Army across the Seven-Mile Creek opposite the Dick Smith Place, near Farmington, which force was vigorously met by a similar force of Confederates. For four or five hours there was a desperate fight, with the Union force at a great disadvantage because of the fact that their only way of approaching was by a narrow road through an impassable swamp. As soon as the Confederates discovered this condition, they brought reënforcements to the point of action, and, by a strong counterattack, drove the enemy back, with a considerable loss of Union men and one battery of guns.

Then, later in May, came the fighting on the Purdy Road, three miles north of Corinth—at the old Dickery field, on the Pea Ridge Road; at the Surratt Place, on Bridge Creek; on the Farmington Road, at the Box Chapel; and on the Burnsville Road, at Shelton Hill, now the poorhouse.

The Union Army was attacking along the entire line, and the general opinion on our side was that the day for a general engagement against Corinth and or entrenchments had come.

Our full force was called to the trenches, and remained in line of battle all day. But it developed afterwards that the enemy was only feeling his way toward our fortifications and gaining the higher points wherever possible, so as to establish his large guns in positions from which he could shell our lines before storming our works with his infantry. General Halleck had made every preparation to capture Corinth. In his final dispositions, heavy mortars had been so placed that they could throw shells into the heart of the town. Rather novel signal stations had been set up by securing high poles to the tops of trees. This enabled the signal corps to overlook the surrounding country, to see our line of entrenchments, and to direct the movements of attacking troops, as well as the fire of the shelling guns.

Just how well General Beauregard had timed the attack of the enemy is shown by the closing events of the siege of Corinth.

For many days our army had been moving out train loads of supplies, and at nightfall on May 29 we were all lined up in the trenches; but as soon as darkness came, everything except the cavalry marched out, bidding a final adieu to Corinth. On the following morning at daybreak, when the enemy advanced his skirmish line, he met with no resistance; and when the first line of battle advanced, it found the trenches deserted.

The regiment of Union troops sent around to the rear to prevent our withdrawal arrived too late, and our trains had all passed when they began removing rails from the tracks.

As General Forrest had been wounded on the way from Shiloh, General Chalmers was in command of all the cavalry which covered our retreat from Corinth to Tupelo, Miss.

CHAPTER 8

BATTLE OF RIENZI

O N May 31, 1862, in covering our retreat from Corinth, we came to a clash with the Union cavalry near Rienzi, Miss. We had advanced with a regiment to a position along a field bordering on a skirt of woods, and our company was detailed to go forward and develop the force he knew was following us. The plan was to fire and fall back on our support, but in rounding a curve in the road we came so suddenly upon a company of the enemy that all preconceived plans were expelled from our excited minds. Our forces were about equal, and we immediately charged. This resulted in a very awkward mix-up for a few minutes. The Union company gave ground, and before we knew what was happening we were face to face with a brigade of Union cavalry. Our plight was precarious indeed. My horse, no less excited than was his rider, carried me wildly for a few yards into the enemy's line.

With the superhuman strength of necessity, I succeeded in turning him, but was forced to run the gantlet of a number of troopers, who, to my good fortune, had exhausted their guns and were using their saber on our men. I was armed with a carbine and two six-shooters. I had already emptied the carbine and one of my pistols. As I neared the getting-out place, I moved as rapidly as a good and thoroughly frightened horse could carry me; but I saw two soldiers moving to close my narrow gap, armed with sabers. I reserved my fire until I was close to them, and then fired point blank at each of them in close succession. I did not tarry to see the full result of my fire, but I know that I stopped their charge on me. I knew that if I could get by them, nothing but a bullet could overtake me.

One of our boys was so closely chased by a Union soldier that the "Yank" was able to freely belabor him with a very dull saber. Finally the Confederate turned and said to his chaser: "Quit hitting me with that thing, you durned fool! Haven't you any better sense than that?" This comrade escaped by strategy and quick action, but his left arm and shoulder were so badly bruised that he was compelled to carry the arm in a "sling" for a month.

This fight occurred near Rienzi, Miss., and was rated by us as only an inconsequential cavalry skirmish; but it later developed that the

Union troop was commanded by Gen. Philip Sheridan, and that he, in honor of this, his first fight and victory, named his war horse "Rienzi." This was the horse which carried him on his celebrated ride at Winchester, Va.

The next day after this fight we retired to Blackland, near Booneville, Miss., and from here our company was sent back on a scouting mission toward Rienzi. Coming suddenly on a picket guard, we captured five or six men gathered at a blacksmith shop, where they were sharpening their sabers on a grindstone. These were among the men we had encountered the day before, and they were not satisfied with their experience in pounding on us with dull weapons.

At Blackland, General Chalmers collected all the Confederate cavalry, with two field batteries, and, selecting an advantageous position, decided to oppose any force that might be following our retreat. Sending out decoys, we tried in vain to draw the enemy into our trap; but our efforts were without avail, as he returned to Corinth and vicinity and our army stopped at Tupelo and went into camp for a little while.

CHAPTER 9

———

MURFREESBORO AND
KENTUCKY CAMPAIGN

———

o meet emergencies at different points, this Grand Army of the Southwest was divided into a number of organizations. General Price, with one part, was sent west of the Mississippi River; one part was sent to Vicksburg; while the largest portion was given to General Bragg to begin his invasion of Kentucky. Forrest, with his troops, marched to Chattanooga, from which point, with his own command, Wharton's Texas Regiment, and a small number from the command of Gen. Joe Wheeler, he made a rapid advance on Murfreesboro, Tenn., where General Crittenden was guarding large stores of military supplies.

Reaching the outskirts of the town about daylight, we chased the pickets into the camp of a Michigan regiment. Pressing rapidly at every point, we soon had everything before us on the run, as our attack was a complete surprise. Our success was absolute, and this capture of a Union division with its commander and the military supplies being guarded was one of the most spectacular strokes of the Civil War.

This attack and capture staged an occurrence which illustrates the tragedy of war. Judge Richardson, for many years after the war a member of Congress from the Huntsville (Ala.) district, some time before our capture of Murfreesboro had been captured near that place; and although he had succeeded in escaping from his captors, he was still inside the Union lines; and so the two traveled together for a day or so until they were recaptured by troops from the garrison and placed in prison at Murfreesboro. It developed after their capture that the companion of Richardson was a spy, or at least the enemy found suspicious papers in his possession; and after a trial, both were sentenced to be shot. This sentence was due to be executed on the morning that our troops rode into Murfreesboro, preventing the death of Richardson and his fellow prisoner. After we had gained possession of the town, the following facts came to light: Richardson and his companion were in a wooden cell, with the death watch over them, when our troops attacked; and when it became evident that we would succeed in capturing the garrison, the Union guard set fire to the house to "see the rebels burn," and the fire was making headway when our advanced troops reached the place and released the prisoners.

After the matter was explained to General Forrest, and Mr. Richardson verified the truth of the story, the General asked Richardson and his companion to identify the guard. The Union prisoners were lined up; and when the two searchers came to the guilty man, he was marched out and shot to death in the presence of both commands after General Forrest had explained the offense to General Crittenden.

After our return to Chattanooga from Murfreesboro, we took the advance of Bragg's army, and on September 14, 1862, appeared in front of the Union fort at Munfordsville, Ky. Then followed a rather ill-timed attack on this strong position, in which our men lost heavily and accomplished very little.

Our cavalry played practically no part in this battle, and I was an onlooker.

After our ineffective attack, the main body of our army came up and captured the garrison.

Then, after feinting in a threatening attitude toward Louisville, we withdrew; and in our southward movement our army encountered General Buell's army, resulting in the battle of Perryville, one of the fiercest struggles of the war. The result of this battle is generally considered a draw, but the immediate advantage was with the Confederates, as our purpose was not stayed, and we continued our retreat to Murfreesboro, Tenn.

During our advance into Kentucky the cavalry was commanded by Col. John H. Morgan. We had a number of fights, captured many soldiers, and destroyed large quantities of military stores.

By the brilliant work of John H. Morgan and N.B. Forrest, cavalry leaders, General Buell was prevented from gaining any hurtful advantage over our retreating and smaller army.

CHAPTER 10

———

THE BATTLE OF CORINTH

———

THE command of General Forrest was not in the battle of Corinth, as it occurred while we were in Kentucky; but because of the sentiment that attaches to the place as my home I desire to record here the substance of a description given me by a kinsman of the Second Texas who was in the battle.

After the battle of Iuka, on September 19 and 20, 1862, the commands of General Price and General Van Dorn were united; and these two commanders resolved to attack Corinth, then occupied by the Union Army under General Rosecrans.

Under the supreme command of General Van Dorn, the Confederate Army left Chewalla, a railroad station eight miles west of Corinth, on the morning of October 3, 1862.

About ten o'clock in the morning the order to attack was given, and the command moved forward cautiously, with its skirmish line deployed in front. In a short time the skirmishers of the Second Texas became engaged with skirmishers of the enemy, and the Forty-Second Alabama Regiment, coming up during the engagement, mistook the Texans for a command of the enemy, and fired upon them, killing Lieutenant Haynes, of Company E., and six private soldiers.

The engagement soon became general. The enemy, however, retreated and fell back beyond the old Confederate breastworks, the same that I had helped to locate before the evacuation of Corinth. As our line advanced, we discovered that the Union Army was making a stand at an entrenched camp, which was strongly fortified. Their resistance was stubborn, but we drove them from their strong position. They did not retire a great distance before making another stand, seemingly with greatly increased numbers. After a brief stand, they charged us. The Second Texas received the shock, and, furiously counter attacking, they cut the Union line and captured some three hundred prisoners. At this juncture several Union batteries opened a tremendous fire on the right of the Texans from an elevated position on the south side of the Memphis and Charleston (now Southern) Railroad. The Second Texas was ordered to charge the batteries. Colonel Rodgers saw that they had been discovered by a brigade of infantry, and asked for reënforcements. Johnson's and Dockery's Arkansas Regiments of Cabell's Brigade were sent, and the three regiments charged, driving back the infantry and capturing three batteries of light artillery.

We next found the stubborn enemy entrenched in a camp on an elevation between two prongs of a creek, where fresh troops had already been massed. Here was presented the most determined stand we had met with during the day. After hard fighting, with heavy losses on both sides, the Union troops were finally driven from this position at the point of the bayonet. The Union officers tried gallantly to stem the tide, General Ogelsby and General Hackelman being desperately wounded in a vain effort to rally their beaten soldiers. In this camp we found bread, butter, cheese, crackers, and other food in abundance, and, while enjoying a short rest, partook of the enemy's unwilling hospitality during his enforced absence—the first food we had tasted that day.

When driven from this position, the enemy fled precipitately to the protection of the inner fortifications at Corinth.

About sunset the exhausted Confederates, with empty cartridge boxes, halted within about a half mile of Corinth and very near the inner fortifications. The loss in our regiment was very heavy. Among the wounded were Lieut.

A.K. Leigh and Halbert Rodgers, the youthful son of the colonel who, during the day, had handled his regiment with consummate skill, being with it in every position of danger.

Before daylight on October 4 the Confederate artillery opened a rigorous fire on the enemy's works, and a lively contest between the gray and blue cannon was kept up until after daylight. During the early morning there was sharp fighting on the skirmish line in front of the Second Texas, in which the Union skirmishers were driven in and their commander, Col. Joseph A. Mower, was severely wounded and captured, but again fell into the hands of his friends that evening after our retreat from Corinth.

Directly in front of the Second Texas, a short distance north of the Memphis and Charleston Railroad, was "Fort Robinette," with three twenty-pound siege guns; and in "Fort Williams," on the south side of the railroad, there were four twenty-four pounders and two eight-inch Howitzers. On the eminence between "Fort Williams" and the railroad were six guns of Battery F., U.S. Light Artillery; and on the south side of the same fort were two guns of the Second Illinois Light Artillery—all commanding the field to the westward and in positions to sweep the hillside in front of "Robinette." In addition to these, two guns of the Wisconsin Light Artillery occupied a point just north of and very close to

"Robinette," between it and the Chewalla dirt road, and in a position to sweep the top and side of the hill in front.

These were the positions of the Union artillery, seventeen guns in all in front of the Second Texas Regiment and commanding the ground over which that wonderful organization of fighters was about to deliver one of the most daring and desperate assaults in the history of wars.

The Union infantry was also placed advantageously for dealing destruction to the assaulting column.

The Forty-Seventh Illinois Regiment lay behind the railroad, immediately in front of "Fort Williams," covering the hillside with their deadly Springfield rifles. The Forty-Third Ohio occupied the ground immediately behind the breastworks on the north side of "Robinette," with its left near the fort. The Eleventh Missouri was lying down under the hill, about fifty yards in the rear of "Robinette," with its right and left wings expanding opposite the Forty-Third and Sixty-Third Ohio, respectively. The Twenty-Seventh Ohio occupied the trenches on the right of the Sixty-Third; and the Thirty-Ninth Ohio was still further to the north, on the right of the Twenty-Seventh, with its right wing facing north, at right angles to the line of its left wing and to the Twenty-Seventh and the Sixty-Third.

The order to charge had been expected every moment since daylight; but owing to the sudden illness of General Herbert, commanding the Left Division of Price's Corps, the initial attack had been delayed until about ten o'clock. During the interval of waiting the men were subjected to the most intense mental strain. As every trained and experienced soldier will testify, the suspense of waiting in the prelude of an onset is more trying than the actual conflict, wherein the heat of battle fevers the mind into a kind of fearless frenzy that causes it to lose the weights and measures of danger.

When the order to advance was given, that fine body of soldiers obeyed as unhesitatingly as if the impulse to move had been that of a single man, the different regiments being massed in five lines of two companies each. When they encountered the abatis—an obstruction of felled trees, with sharpened and interwoven branches—the formation was necessarily somewhat broken, just as the enemy's artillery began to blast and wither the moving mass of men; but each man, though but an atom of the fiery storm, moved with a separate though strangely cooperative intelligence, advancing with remarkable rapidity toward the common objective, "Fort Robinette." As soon as the abatis was passed, a partial restoration of the organizations took place in the very furnace of battle as the lines sprang forward with a many-voiced yell. When they reached the brow of the hill, the earth trembled under the deafening crash of the opposing artillery, while the Union infantry regiments poured a deadly enfilading fire into the right flank of the Texans. It was beyond power of human endurance, however sublime the courage that willed it, to withstand such a shock of lead and iron, and the attackers of "Robinette" recoiled through a quivering sheet of flame. With encouraging words from the intrepid colonel, a partial reformation was effected, and the order to charge again was given. As steel on flint, a blow to the brave strikes fire in the soul; and so these smitten Texans flamed with fury as they returned to the charge. The slaughter was one-sided and terrible; and as the men in gray recoiled a second time, the fourth color bearer fell with the flag in his hand. Then it was that Colonel Rodgers seized the tattered banner and rode into the midst of his heroic band. Once more forming them into a ragged line, he asked if they were willing to follow him, and they responded with an affirmative yell. Again the order to advance was given, and the Colonel rode up the hill directly toward the fort, bearing the colors.

With a steady gaze fixed on the fort, he moderated his horse's pace to the pace of his men. The column moved forward in double-quick time. Their ranks were ruthlessly raked with lead and iron; but the living filled the gaps left by the dead, as the bleeding remnant pressed on to the fort.

Colonel Rodgers rode into the ditch that fronted the works, followed by the head of his column; and as the others came up, they scattered around either side. The right wing of the Second Texas was met by the determined front of the Forty-Third Ohio, and a hand-to-hand conflict followed. The onset of the Texans was made with such reckless desperation that the Ohioans were put to flight, leaving one-half of their number killed or wounded on the ground, their brave colonel, J. Kirby-Smith, being among the slain.

On the north side of "Robinette" the left wing of the Second Texas came in contact with the Sixty-Third Ohio; and, after a bloody contest at close quarters, the blue column was driven back at the point of the bayonet, leaving fifty-three per cent of its number on the ground. The section of light artillery at that point made its escape to the Union rear.

While these bloody conflicts were taking place on both flanks of the fort, Colonel Rodgers climbed upon the parapet and planted the flag of his regiment in triumph at its top. The men who had followed him leaped fearlessly down inside the fort, and, with others who had crawled through the embrasures, unexpectedly engaged the cannoneers in a hand-to-hand conflict. The fight was short and fierce, and thirteen out of twenty-six men of the First U.S. Infantry who manned the guns of the fort were slain, and a number of others, including the commander, Lieutenant Robinette, were wounded.

Thus was the fort captured and silenced; but "Fort Williams" continued to pour its deadly fire into the gray, thinned ranks and into the struggling mass of gray and blue, while the Forty-Seventh Illinois, from its elevated position along the railroad, swept the parapets of "Robinette" with long-range rifles as the Confederates scaled them.

Meantime a fearful hand-to-hand fight was raging in the heart of the town—around the railroad depot, the Tishomingo Hotel, the Corinth House, and even in the yard around the headquarters of General Rosecrans, the old Duncan homestead. The fighting was furious, but the heavy reserves of fresh troops which the Union commander had massed in the central and the southwest portions of the town met the torn and half-exhausted columns of the Confederates and literally plucked victory from defeat.

The victorious reserves of the enemy marched upon "Robinette" from the town, Gen. David S. Stanley advancing from the southeast

with the reformed Forty-Third Ohio and two
fresh regiments.

When it was apparent to the little band of
Texans in and upon the captured fort that their
dearly bought victory was of no avail and that
the day was lost with the repulse of the Confederates in the center of the town, Colonel
Rodgers' first thought was to save the lives of
as many of his men as possible, and he waved
his handkerchief from the top of the parapet,
making known his desire to surrender; but the
enemy either did not see him or misunderstood
or mistrusted the signal, for the firing continued from both advancing columns. He then said
to the men around him: "The enemy refuses to
accept our surrender, and we will see our lives
as dearly as possible."

With a calm precision, he then ordered his
men to fall back into the ditch outside the fort,
and there gave the order for the retreat. He
climbed out of the ditch with the flag in one
hand and his pistol in the other, the remnant of
his shattered band clustering around him, and
they slowly retreated backward as they returned
the fire of the advancing and overwhelming
lines of blue.

Up to this time the Eleventh Missouri Regiment had not fired a shot; but about the time
this heroic retreat began, it suddenly rose from
its waiting position, rushed upon and round the

fort, and poured a withering fire into the retreat-ing band of Texans, and their intrepid leader fell, pierced with eleven wounds. The flag fell across his body; and the few yet remaining of his loyal band, remembering the vows made when this flag was presented to the regiment at Houston by the ladies of Texas, seized and bore the fallen emblem away, Ben Wade, of Company I, being the man who rescued it.

By this time the whole Confederate Army was in retreat. General Villepigue's Brigade of Lovell's Division marched by the left flank across the Memphis and Charleston Railroad and threw its columns between the shattered ranks of Maury's Division and the expected pursuit. The conquerors stood aghast at the combination of circumstances which had given them the vic-tory. Enchanted by the comparative calm that followed the storm, they seemed satisfied to rest upon their laurels and forego the opportunity to follow the weary and beaten foe.

When the smoke lifted its somber veil from the sorrowful field of carnage, the face of the landscape was distorted with horror, expressed in suffering and death. But the spirit of immor-tal glory hovered there, for the soil of Missis-sippi had been sanctified by the blood of heroes, and amid the falling tears and broken hearts of the South and of the North the Muse of His-tory was gathering from the broken circles of death-smitten homes names for the roll of eternal flame.

The whole century was electrified by the news of the fearless assault of Rodgers and his Texans. Illustrated papers of the North carried pictures of the dramatic scenes.

In closing his report of the battle, General Van Dorn said: "I cannot refrain from mentioning here the conspicuous gallantry of a noble Texan whose deeds at Corinth are the constant theme of both friends and foes. As long as courage, manliness, fortitude, patriotism, and honor exist, the name of Rodgers will be revered and honored among men. He fell in the front of battle and died beneath the colors of his regiment in the very center of the enemy's stronghold. He sleeps, and Glory is his sentinel."

The deeds of this brave officer called forth not only the encomium of his commanding general, but also the approval and admiration of the big-hearted commander of the Union Army. By order of General Rosecrans, the body of the fallen hero was buried with military honors upon the field where he fell and the grave inclosed with wooden palings.

What sadder illustration of War's ruthless waste of manhood could there be than is presented in the sacrificial death of that heroic son of Texas? What a wealth of courage, integrity, and high purpose that might have been utilized in the bloodless battles of a nation's peaceful progress was forced to perish under the juggernaut of fraternal strife! What a scathing indictment of our civilization—our politics, our religion— is that lonely grave!

Among the officers killed were Colonel Rodgers, Second Texas; Colonel Johnston, Twentieth Arkansas; Major James, Twentieth Arkansas; Col. J.D. Martin, commanding the Fourth Brigade of Price's Division.

CHAPTER II

———

WEST TENNESSEE

———

A FTER coming out of the campaign of Kentucky, the cavalry forces were employed to harass the enemy; and after the lapse of nearly sixty years, it is exhilarating to my imagination to recall the wondrous part played by General Forrest and his comparatively small command in that great game of life and death.

While Morgan's command was striking the key points of the Louisville and Nashville Railroad to hamper the supply lines of Rosecrans at Nashville, Forrest was performing the same service against the Mobile and Ohio and the Memphis and Charleston, the supply lines of the enemy at Corinth, Miss.

Leaving Chattanooga late in November, he hurried to West Tennessee, crossing the Tennessee River at Clifton and pushing hurriedly on to the Mobile and Ohio Railroad line. In rapid succession he engaged and captured the garrisons of Jackson, Humboldt, Trenton, and Spring Creek, with large supplies of arms and food.

In the same campaign we captured the garrison of Lexington, Tenn., and, incidentally, Col. Robert G. Ingersoll, who in later years became the great outstanding orator of the nation and its most brilliant agnostic, or free religious thinker.

On account of the smallness of his command, General Forrest could only hope to succeed by rapidity of movement; and this necessitated the destruction of all captured property and the paroling of all prisoners.

Only a commander of genius and boldness could have coped with such a situation as confronted Forrest. The territory in which he operated was in the hands of the enemy, both lines of railroad controlled and guarded by the Union armies. On the east was the Tennessee River, deep and cold, and, ever hovering on its turbulent waters, a fleet of gunboats, such as had carried terror to Henry and Donelson and Shiloh.

Thus hemmed within the encircling barriers of the Tennessee, the Ohio, the Mississippi, and the army of Grant, this fearless Murat of the Confederacy moved at will, a veritable flying scourge of death and destruction, while the surprised and startled enemy made hasty and widespread preparation for his capture; but the reincarnated spirit of the Cavaliers rode as they reckoned, and, as in the movements of all truly great commanders, the unexpected happened.

At a place called "Parker Cross-Roads," opposite and west of Clifton, on the Tennessee, the Union Army had a division of infantry and artillery about to be reinforced by a brigade then on its way from Union City by the Mobile and Ohio Railroad.

We were put in line of battle and ordered to an immediate attack against the Parker Cross-Roads force, a portion of his command attacking in the rear, while that portion with which I was fighting attacked the front. Meantime a regiment had been sent to meet the column coming from Union City. The Cross-Roads fight was waged in the open, and, considering the numbers engaged, was as fierce and bloody as Shiloh or Perryville.

In the confusion resulting from being attacked front and rear, without any knowledge of our numbers, the enemy, under a flag of truce sent by General Forrest, with a demand for surrender, was undoubtedly at the point of yielding, when a lightning-like surprise broke the calm where the fighting has ceased.

The Union column from Union City had missed our regiment sent to meet them and had attacked our horse holders without warning and driven them in great confusion into our fighting ranks. Hurriedly, General Forrest concentrated his entire force, turned the horse holders into fighters, and placed a small guard around the horses.

We immediately charged the newcomers and put them to flight, and then headed for the Tennessee River. We never knew nor stopped to inquire what the enemy, so near to the point of surrender, thought of our sudden withdrawal.

When we had crossed the river on our way in, we had sunk our boats and left them cabled, so that we could use them on the return; so, by working all night, we recrossed with artillery and full command and drew safely away from the zone of danger, only to enter another.

It is not necessary to the discerning reader to comment upon the genius of Forrest displayed in this campaign. Great danger seemed to sharpen his abilities and make surer his success.

CHAPTER 12

MIDDLE TENNESSEE

AFTER our return from this raid, we rejoined Bragg's army near Murfreesboro, Tenn.; and Generals Wheeler and Forrest took all the cavalry and made a raid on Fort Donelson. Against General Forrest's judgment, General Wheeler, the senior in command, decided to attack the garrison. With heavy loss, we were repulsed, and retired without accomplishing anything.

Our next move was to join the forces of General Van Dorn in Middle Tennessee; and on March 5, 1863, we surrounded Thompson's Station, on the Louisville and Nashville Railroad, and, after a sharp fight, captured the garrison and 1,306 men, including the two commanders, Colonels Coburn and W.R. Shafter. The latter was a conspicuous general in the Spanish-American War of 1898.

We spent March fighting detachments in and around Franklin, Tenn. On March 25 we captured Brentwood and destroyed the bridge over Harpeth River between Franklin and Nashville.

Here I had another close call. The Union Army had sent out a large force after us and has succeeded in getting between a part of our command and the river, forcing us to ford at a point extremely dangerous. We were fighting as we ran and were compelled to jump our horses from a high embankment into the river. My horse carried me under to a great depth; but he was not disabled, and, by great exertion, came up and swam across. Some of our men were drowned, and many were shot by the enemy as the mass of men and horses struggled in the river.

I had read, as a boy, the thrilling story of Israel Putnam's reckless ride over a precipice, but I never dreamed that I would one day be forced to the same extremity.

In the hard school of war I learned that, under the stress of great danger, a man, in mind and body, will perform the unbelievable.

After making our get-away from Harpeth River, on April 10, we had another fight at Franklin, Tenn., capturing the enemy's wagon train, two cannon, and a number of prisoners. We then returned to Bragg's army in the vicinity of Chattanooga.

CHAPTER 13

PURSUIT OF THE
STREIGHT RAIDERS

L ATE in April came news that the Union Army around Corinth was making a demonstration into North Alabama.

Forrest's genius had already become known, and he was sent with 800 men to uncover the design of the enemy.

When we arrived in the vicinity of Tuscumbia, Ala., we found a part of General Roddy's Confederate command fighting and retreating before the advancing enemy from near Cherokee.

On reaching Tuscumbia, Forrest sent out scouts in all directions to ascertain the purpose of the enemy. Upon the reports of these scouts, Forrest understood the general plan of the foe.

Col. A.D. Streight, in command of an Indiana regiment of infantry, was to raid through Alabama and on to Rome, Ga., cutting the railway and destroying factories.

But—alas for the plan!—General Forrest did not remain in Middle Tennessee, where they had placed him.

Learning from a citizen that Streight's column had passed the little town of Mount Hope, only a few miles from Tuscumbia, on the evening of April 29, Forrest ordered every available man with a good horse to prepare for the pursuit. With 500 of his own men and 800 from Roddy's command, he began the chase with 1,300 men and with Streight twelve hours ahead.

Forrest's calculation was that Streight would camp at the base of Sand Mountain and begin the ascent early the next day, and so it was. Just at sunrise our advance guard came on the enemy's pickets. The army was breaking camp as we came into view, and a chorus of 2,000 braying mule voices greeted us, as Streight's men were mounted on mules for mountain climbing.

We were a little too late to strike the enemy in camp according to plan, but a hasty and too eager company of our advance rushed in and fired on the rear of the column; whereupon the enemy turned and fought back, holding us off until he got his force on top of the mountain. Then he placed his men back in ambush and drew us into a deadly trap. In a rushing movement we were surprised and knocked out of all formation. It was the only time in my entire service of four years with Forrest that I ever saw

him perturbed. He tried with all possible boldness to stem the tide; but our men had ridden
hard all night, and they simply could not meet
the advantage and the odds of fresh troops.

After losing a number of men, we "stood
not upon the order of our going," but recoiled
from the front of flame; and on our retreat the
enemy pursued us so closely that we lost two of
our field pieces. Our retreat so enraged General Forrest that he was as ferocious and wild as
a lion. He was so harsh in his treatment of the
young captain of artillery on account of the loss
of his guns that he afterwards, at Spring Hill,
Tenn., attacked and shot General Forrest.

After this repulse, we brought up the remainder of our troops and turned the pursuit and
kept it up so vigorously that they soon began
to try to get away from us, and we pressed the
running fight until we put these 2,000 raiders
out of business.

After this fight of Day's Gap, on Sand Mountain, followed that long and relentless pursuit
of Streight and his men, which must forever
stand as one of the most daring and spectacular
exploits of military history. Forrest had picked
500 men for this great running fight with a foe
2,000 strong.

Our fight was, of course, with the rear guard,
for our leader never permitted us to be drawn
into a general engagement.

When the enemy would set traps for us, Forrest would invariably discover them and shell the ambush out and keep up his nagging, sleep-destroying pursuit day and night.

It was in the course of this pursuit that we came to the deep, high-banked waters of Black Warrior Creek and found the enemy on the opposite bank and the bridge in flames.

Near the burning bridge lived the Widow Sanson, whose fifteen-year-old daughter, Emma Sanson, made her name immortal in the records of the Southern Confederacy and in the sacred, tear-stained archives of Alabama. She it was who rode on Forrest's horse behind him through the zone of danger to point out a little-known and isolated ford where she had seen her mother's cows cross when the summer waters were low. By her timely help Forrest was enabled to pursue the enemy's column in its last stretch of the long march to Rome.

For this intelligent, fearless, and patriotic service, her State, after the war, granted to Emma Sanson a section of land and in 1907 erected a monument to her memory at Gadsden.

Before Streight's column reached Rome, Ga., Forrest sent a courier around the flying foe and called upon the city officials to raise a force and seize the bridge and either hold or burn it. The response was prompt, and the Union commander found a hostile reception awaiting him and the bridge barricaded and guarded with cannon.

Our advance arrived within striking distance of the enemy's rear just as he received the word that the city had refused to surrender, and so the really courageous Union commander, after reaching the edge of his goal, surrendered his nearly 2,000 soldiers to Forrest's little band of less than 500.

With chagrin and humiliation, Colonel Streight learned too late the strength of the column that had harassed his troops over so many hills, and then compelled them to stack arms.

While I was but a unit of that swift band, my experience brought to my understanding the awful tragedy of war and taught me the strange truth that the will and the genius of the commander are the preponderant power of every bannered host, the fineness of a brain cell, the courage of a heart, the coolness of a nerve, outweighing the mass of legions.

Soon after this we marched back to Bragg's army in Tennessee. We were sent out on scout service toward Nashville, and fought a number of minor engagements, including those of Tullahoma and Shelbyville, Tenn. After a little while, we joined Wheeler's command; and our activities were then directed against the forces of Generals Wilder and Stanley, who were making strenuous efforts to cut the Western and Atlantic Railroad line, Bragg's line of communication.

CHAPTER 14

CHICKAMAUGA

F OLLOWING soon after these scattered raids came the great battle of Chickamauga, which is too well known to the world to need comment from me.

Forrest's cavalry virtually opened the battle of Chickamauga; and after the field seemed won by the Confederates, General Forrest climbed a tree and observed the confusion with which the Union lines were retiring. Upon this knowledge, he boldly urged General Bragg to press on after the foe, and pressed him so vehemently and so undiplomatically that, it is said, General Bragg severely reprimanded him for what Bragg considered an undue interference with matters under the authority of his superior. The story further runs that General Forrest's attitude, following the incident, was such that a duel would have resulted had it not been for General Bragg's cool disregard of General Forrest's desire to bring the matter to a violent conclusion. It is a regrettable fact that this breach between two of the South's ablest and noblest sons was never healed.

I believe that time and impartial history have proved that if General Bragg had followed the advice of Forrest at Chickamauga, victory, so far as human vision can tell, would have been with the Confederates.

CHAPTER 15

WEST TENNESSEE

FTER the battle of Chickamauga, Forrest, with 300 picked men, turned toward Mississippi to begin the recruiting for his third army. By December 1 we had quite an army of raw recruits, but they were poorly mounted and many of them unarmed. Up to this time Forrest had depended upon his enemy for arms and supplies; and as there was no foe in immediate striking distance, he determined to march through North Mississippi into West Tennessee, then entirely in the hands of the enemy and guarded by a large army, with strong garrisons at Corinth, Miss.; Memphis, Bolivar, and Union City, Tenn. General Hurlbut, the commander of the department, had announced that if Forrest should return he would surely be captured.

About December 1, 1863, we left Holly Springs, Miss., on our northward march. Making the greatest possible display of his force, at the proper time Forrest pushed across the Memphis and Charleston Railroad, left a small force of Mississippi troops to threaten Memphis and Collierville, and moved rapidly on with his main body, reaching Jackson, Tenn., in the very center of Hurlbut's nest, before the enemy knew that Forrest was back in his old haunts. Operating in and around Jackson through December, we added about 2,000 men to our force and collected many beef cattle. The enemy, no realizing that this force was commanded by Forrest, never sought to molest us within our limited area, but awaited the time for our get-away, confident of being able to crush and capture us. The Union forces had already captured John Morgan, and they now felt that Forrest was within their grasp.

On January 1, 1864, we began our movement southward, threatening in all directions, but moving toward the Hatchie River at a point above Bolivar, Tenn. The enemy had failed to find a boat which we had sunk in this stream. At Jack's Creek we encountered the Bolivar force, and easily pushed it back, allowing our main column to pass on to the crowing place on the Hatchie.

Forrest posted a regiment in front of the Bolivar army and gave them orders to fight to the last if necessary, to hold the enemy until we could cross the river. It took us all night. The enemy had made a desperate fight with our rear guard just at sundown but withdrew their line at night and reported to their commander that they had hemmed us in a bend of the stream where we had no means of crossing. They had sent a regiment across the river, and it had gone into camp in a cornfield about a mile from our crossing place.

Forrest had distributed his 300 veterans among the new troops in order to instruct them as to what was expected of them.

After we were safely across the Hatchie followed one of those daring feats of our General so difficult to understand from a description in cold type—so peculiar to his originality on the battlefield. Instead of hurling a heavy force against the regiment camping in the cornfield, he attacked them with his picked escort of eighty men, scattering them to give the impression of a full regiment. With ten special captains giving loud commands, as if company after company were moving to the attack, our thin line dashed upon the sleeping foe in the darkness just before daylight and put the entire regiment to flight mainly with our six-shooters. Forrest did not wish to be burdened with prisoners just as this time, and so he planned to frighten this regiment out of the pathway of his army and secure as many of their horses as possible. The plan succeeded, and we lost only three men, one of them being the gallant "Nathan Boone," commander of the escort.

Many of our men were given good mounts from the number captured. My horse was slightly wounded, and I exchanged him for a large, fine animal which I named "Hatch," "in memory" of a Union colonel commanding a regiment at Bolivar.

Our difficulties grew with our progress. An army of 30,000 men, divided into four divisions, was pressing us on all sides. We had to cross Wolf River and the Memphis and Charleston Railroad, and our force did not exceed 5,000 or 6,000 men, many of them neither armed nor mounted. We were burdened with a drove of beef cattle, our supply wagons, and artillery. General Forrest's plans were known neither to the enemy nor to his own men, and all we could guess was that he would do the unexpected.

Then, while threatening a crossing of the railroad between Collierville and LaGrange, Tenn., with a swiftness that was incredible, our main column pushed out toward Rossville and Memphis, as if to attack the latter. We crossed the Wolf River near Rossville, putting the guard to flight and reflooring the partially wrecked bridge with fence rails. We then dispersed the force between us and the railroad and defeated the division which opposed us at the railroad, thus, with the loss of not more than thirty men, escaping the wrathful meshes of a force five times our number.

It had been said that "comparisons are odious," but it is a living truth that values exist only in comparison; and the military student cannot fail to retrace the immortal campaigns of Alexander, Hannibal, Caesar, Frederick, and Napoleon in the lightning-like, yet perfectly timed, movements of this untrained, unpolished genius of war, now known to history as Nathan Bedford Forrest.

The enemies of General Forrest were the first to recognize his great and dangerous ability as West Pointer after West Pointer toppled before his flying column.

After this raid it is said that General Sherman, more than any of the other Union commanders, saw and appreciated the danger of this untutored captain of the Confederacy, and that he openly declared that the commander who could vanquish or capture Forrest would be made a major general in addition to receiving a reward of fifty thousand dollars.

CHAPTER 16

———

GEN. "SOOEY" SMITH

———

THE first try for the Sherman reward was Gen. "Sooey" Smith, a West Pointer and a brave soldier.

After the return from our raid of 1864, our command was scattered from Okolona to West Point, Miss., for the purpose of recruiting and organizing for a greater campaign; but while we were thus scattered, General Smith pounced upon us with a choice of brigade of well-armed and well-equipped soldiers.

Of course, General Forrest had our reconnoitering parties at all times to forestall a possible surprise, and it was while out with one of these parties that I had one of the most thrilling experiences of my entire service. We had been informed by a citizen sheriff as to the location of a command of hostile soldiers. Before going with this sheriff to a point from which he said we could see into the Union camp, he invited us to rest and feed our horses in a secluded thicket where he had hidden his own stock. He did not know that his negro caretaker had deserted to the enemy, but such was the case; and while we were enjoying our rest, we were suddenly attacked and almost surrounded. When the sheriff saw the situation, he begged us not to fire on the intruders, in fear of the possible consequence to the community, and so we saved ourselves in flight as best we could. I was so closely pressed by a trooper, firing at me at close range, that I could not mount my horse; and in some way, not clear to me, I escaped into the woods, followed by a shower of bullets which I suppose I outran. My good horse "Hatch" was gone, and, with him, the brace of six-shooters which I had captured from Major Phillips before the evacuation of Corinth.

With a heavy heart, I left my hiding place at sunset, and, with all possible haste, concentrated my thought and energies in an effort to reach some citizen who would furnish me a mount that I might take word of the approaching enemy to my command. With but little delay, I succeeded in securing a beautiful, but blind, little horse. With minute directions from his owner as to my route to Okolona, I set out; and as the enemy had gone into camp for the night, I outstripped him and gave the news first to the detachment at Okolona and then to General

Forrest, who, with the main force, was further on toward West Point. Whether or not General Forrest had previously formed his plan in anticipation of an attack, we knew not; but its execution was as swift as if it had been slated in advance, instructing the Okolona force to fight and slowly fall back upon the main column, lying along a creek near West Point. This creek was a low, sluggish stream; and at this time its swollen waters were covering the adjacent bottom lands, forming a wide marsh, spanned by a single road and a narrow bridge, making a new-world Arcola for this new Napoleon of the Confederacy. A fine decoy had been the Okolona retreating troops, as they had brought General Smith's army to the exact spot where General Forrest had desired to meet it.

On February 20 the enemy lined up for battle and attacked our troops near the Tibbee Creek. The fight was fast and furious at the beginning. The enemy could not understand the sudden resistance after having chased the Okolona column so successfully.

Forrest held his veteran soldiers and his artillery in reserve until the enemy was well within his trap. To us it looked at one time as though our leader had made a mistake, as our advanced line was pressed so vigorously that it fell back in confusion. General Forrest in person rallied the retreating Confederates; and after a fierce rebuke to some of his fleeing soldiers, he lined up his escort and commanded that the troops follow this company. This was the word for a full attack, in which we turned the tide of battle and sent the enemy staggering back on his reserve. Forrest did not give the enemy time to reform but pressed on into his broken ranks with such vigor that the Union Army was scattered out of all organization and fled from the field, utterly confused.

We kept up the chase until the enemy made a stand at a hill just north of Okolona on the Pontotoc Road. The commander massed his men on a steep and rugged hillside and gave us a hard, game fight. Jeffrey Forrest, a brother of our General, was killed here on February 24, and this sad incident so aroused Forrest that he seemed to lose all sense of personal danger. At the head of McCullough's regiment, he charged the enemy from his position, and got so far in advance of his own men that we found him in the midst of the Union rear guard, fighting off his enemies from all sides. Colonel McCullough hastened to his assistance and extricated him from his perilous position. After this fight the enemy made no further effort to hold us in check but gave all his thought and energy to a rapid retreat back to Memphis.

CHAPTER 17

———

FORT PILLOW

———

ON March 1, 1864, we began another invasion of West Tennessee; but as the active troops in that section had been reduced to a few strong garrisons, we did not meet any serious opposition until we came to the vicinity of Fort Pillow, just above Memphis. Pillow was garrisoned with negro soldiers commanded by white officers. This place being considered almost impregnable, it was used as a recruiting station and a supply base.

Up to that time the Union commanders had looked upon Forrest as being only cavalry raider and running fighter; but, in truth, his command was mounted infantry, with two full batteries of artillery, and at this time it was composed of veteran troops.

The enemy had too much faith in the impregnability of the fort and too little regard for the genius of N.B. Forrest.

There has been so much misrepresentation regarding the capture of Fort Pillow and it was, at the time, such a football of prejudice that I think the truth should be told by an unbiased statement of the facts.

Our army approached Fort Pillow about the 12th of April and drove in the outpost guards, and, after a sharp fight with the outside defenders, we forced the enemy behind the fortifications. The Union Army had a transport boat and one or more gunboats in the river and could fear no attack from that side of the fort. Our commander, knowing the danger of a direct assault and the heavy loss of life that would be sure to follow, sent in a flag of truce demanding capitulation, making it plain that he had come to capture the fort and assuring the defenders that the terms to be granted would be honorable. He warned them, however, that if his men had to scale the walls of the fort he could not guarantee full protection to the negro soldiers in view of the Southern white man's strong prejudice against the colored man as a soldier at that period of the war.

There have been many wild stories concocted about this fight; but aside from the outcropping of natural race prejudice, which is dangerous enough under normal, peaceful conditions of life and which had been blown to its fiercest flame by the breath of war, there was nothing brutal or savage.

Just before our flag of truce went forward, one of our regiments slipped into a ravine just above the fort, where they were safe from the enemy's fire and from which position they could enfilade the fort and boat landing.

Soon after the fight the report was current that this regiment had been moved into position while the flag of truce was being respected.

Another story that gained circulation, and that has believers to this day, was to the effect that our command murdered all the occupants of the fort; and that fight in which our army took all the hazards of a difficult and dangerous attack was widely called the "massacre of Fort Pillow."

After the war, a committee composed of Northern men investigated these charges against General Forrest and his command, and, upon all information gathered, the accused were, by the decision of the committee, cleared of the charge.

In every army there are bad men, and of such we may expect fiendish conduct when the business of the best of men is to kill.

When we fought it out at Fort Pillow and were forced to scale the walls and found the negro troops defending the place with death-dealing weapons in their hands, I am sure that, in the flame of prejudice and passion, there were some unnecessary killings; but they were the exceptions and formed no part of any plan of the Confederate commander. Neither did they reflect the will and spirit of the mass of his soldiers.

A great many of the panic-stricken negroes ran toward the river, and some were drowned by jumping into the water in an effort to reach the transport, which in alarm was pulling away from the shore. In the stampede there were many who paid no attention when they were called upon to halt, and this gave our men the right under the rules of war to shoot.

CHAPTER 18

———

A PERSONAL SORROW

———

AFTER my return from this fight, it was my lot to undergo the saddest experience of my war life.

My brother, one year my junior, had just joined the command, when we went with a scouting party toward the railroad and met a small party of Union soldiers. It was the first time my brother had been on the firing line. He and I were on the extreme left of the line on the edge of a road, in touch with each other, and we received the first fire from the enemy. He was killed instantly and never spoke, but looked straight at me, with a silent understanding reflected in his eyes, and I caught him as he fell. The ball that killed him struck near his heart and passed through his body. I wrapped his body in a blanket and carried it sixty miles until I reached the main column. Then Gen. S.D. Lee furnished me an ambulance, and I carried the body to Pontotoc, Miss., for burial. After the war I placed a monument over the grave of this beloved brother and youthful soldier.

We had always been as twins, being so nearly the same age, and his tragic and pathetic passing from life left in my heart a burning scar which the long years, with their submerging floods of joy and sorrow, have never wiped out.

This tragedy also left within me a question which time has never answered: Was it by unguided chance or the immutable decree of an unknown Fate that I was permitted to live through fifty-two battles—to survive every kind of danger to which a soldier may be subjected—while this boy by my side, found swift death in his first battle line? Only the Great Commander of all life knows the deep secret of this sad disparity. Speaking from the earthly standpoint from which we judge the tragedies of this world, I was the favored one, as I stood unscathed beside the crumpling body of my beloved brother on that far-distant day, now nearly sixty years gone; but when the light eternal shall unveil the secrets of this fleeting existence, perchance I shall learn that it was a stern Fate that, on that eventful morning, left me the long, long road to travel, while the gentle soul of that boy was borne from the spot of his patriotic sacrifice, to the rewards that are promised, on wings far swifter than the bullet which dissolved the functions of his bodily life.

CHAPTER 19

BATTLE OF
BRICE'S CROSS-ROADS

I N the beginning of the spring of 1864 it
became very necessary that the granaries of
South Mississippi and Alabama should be carefully guarded against a raid from the Union
forces, these sections being absolutely essential
to the sustenance of the Confederate armies.
The task of protecting this land of plenty was
assigned to General Forrest.

When General Sherman was pressing back
the Confederate Army under General Joseph E.
Johnston, he told his people at Washington that
they must keep General Forrest from following
his rear; also that the crops of South Mississippi
and Alabama should be destroyed.

Accordingly, the Union commander at Memphis, Tenn., was ordered to assemble the largest
possible force and place it under an able commander, so that Forrest could be permanently
disposed of.

The force, when assembled on June 1, 1864, consisted of 3,500 cavalry, under two veteran commanders, Grierson and Warring, and 4,500 infantry, under McMillen, Hogue, and Bouton, the latter commanding a regiment of negroes. This army carried 250 wagons and twenty pieces of artillery.

The supreme command was given to Gen. Samuel D. Sturgis, an experienced warrior and brave fighter.

To meet this force, General Forrest had about 5,000 mounted troops, with two batteries of artillery—Morton's and Rice's.

The Federal Army left Memphis on June 1 for Ripley, Miss. Upon reaching that point, they halted and sent a cavalry force east to Hatchie River, and circulated the report that they intended to strike the Mobile and Ohio Railroad at Corinth, Rienzi, or Booneville, and then advance south or go east and cover General Sherman's rear while he was pressing Johnston back through Georgia.

Of course this was done to mislead Forrest, hoping that he would throw his force as far north as Corinth, leaving the enemy time to march his force to Brice's Cross-Roads, in which position he would block the Confederates and force them out through North Alabama, leaving open to Sturgis the rich country of South Mississippi and Alabama, which he so earnestly desired to reach. But Forrest never reached conclusions upon appearances, especially when he had reasons for believing that appearances were being made to deceive. On the 8th of June his command was strung out between Baldwyn, Booneville, Rienzi, and Corinth, Miss., as he was not yet certain as to what his foe contemplated in the invasion of this territory. It was naturally expected that some new tactics would be put forth by the new Union commander.

General Forrest came to our command at Baldwyn and called for a reliable squad of four or five scouts who knew the country through the Hatchie Hills. I was one of the number furnished, and the General called us before him and told us that the Union commander was circulating the report that he was crossing the Hatchie River at Kellum's Mill, and that they were going to Corinth, Miss., as soon as their infantry and artillery came up. Forrest told us that he wanted positive and exact information on this point, and that we must go until we could secure it; that we must not come back with a report that someone had told us so and so, but that we must go until we could see the enemy and know as a fact that they were there in force as represented.

Under these exacting instructions, we set forth, and reached the vicinity of the mill about dark. We went through the woods after we had passed the picket post, and carefully approached the miller's house that stood on the hill over-looking the river.

It was late at night when we reached the house; but our pilot was well acquainted with the family, and they readily told us that the enemy had a pontoon bridge across the river, and that at sundown of that evening there was a brigade of cavalry on each side of the stream; but as General Forrest had told us to go until we could see for ourselves, we mounted and rode down to the bridge. We felt sure that we could ride in among the enemy and secure our information without betraying our presence if we had no mishap. In case we were discovered, we could fire on anyone attacking us, and in the confusion and the darkness we could escape. But when we reached the bridge, there were neither soldiers nor horses to be found, though there were vis-ible evidences of the very recent presence of a large body of horsemen on the ground.

The Union troopers had evidently left at nightfall and had gone to Ripley to join their main column for the march toward Brice's Cross-Roads. As soon as our captain made this discovery, he sent me back to Booneville to tell General Forrest what was transpiring, and that the captain and the other scouts would follow and endeavor to, overtake the enemy and report later the number of the different organizations.

I left Kellum Mill about midnight of June 8, had a hard and lonely ride, and reached Booneville about noon of the 9th, almost exhausted, as was my horse. I found General Forrest occupying an old warehouse as headquarters, and reported to him. He asked me several pointed questions, and, as soon as my message was delivered, he dismissed me and told me to take nourishment and rest—an order which I obeyed very punctually.

Before I got out of the building I heard the General issuing orders for immediate preparation for marching.

At this date our forces were located as follows:

Bell's Brigade was at Rienzi, twenty-five miles from Brice's Cross-Roads.

Rucker's Brigade, with Morton's and Rice's Batteries, was at Booneville, eighteen miles from Brice's Cross-Roads.

The brigade of Lyon and Johnston was Baldwyn, six miles from Brice's Cross-Roads.

General Forrest had instructed all commanders to be in readiness to march on Brice's Cross-Roads at daylight on the morning of June 10. He knew that the enemy heavily outnumbered him, and that General Sturgis was bending every effort to outmarch him to that point in order that he might force the Confederates to attack at a great disadvantage.

It had been raining for some time, and on the night of June 9 there was almost a deluge.

Late in the afternoon of the 9th I was unable to locate my company, as I had left it at Baldwyn; so I rode out toward Blackland and secured lodging in a farmhouse that belonged to a former comrade, and had a good supper and a comfortable night of rest. I found that General Lyon, of the Kentucky Brigade, was spending the night under the same kindly roof.

At daylight of the 10th everything in Forrest's command was on the move. The clouds lifted and the day grew intensely hot.

The Union commander, evidently feeling that he had the situation well in hand, was not so zealous in getting all of his command to the Cross-Roads.

The enemy camped on the night of the 9th of June at Stub's farm, nine miles from the battlefield, while the bulk of our force was twenty miles away. Sturgis sent forward his two brigades of cavalry and took possession of the Cross-Roads, throwing forward a strong force on the Baldwyn and Guntown Road. I marched with General Lyon's force until we met General Forrest with escort, and then I fell in with the escort. We marched rapidly until we struck the Union pickets about three miles out on the Baldwyn Road. There we pressed back until we came up on Warring's Brigade, posted behind a rail fence around a small field of corn. One organization of this command was armed with Colts' repeating rifles, the most dangerous weapon the war had developed up to that time. Forrest, with only about 800 of his men at hand and facing 3,500 men, knew the danger of bringing on a fight. The units of his army were scattered far back on the muddy roads, moving with all possible swiftness to the field. Never did the infinite boldness of Forrest stand out more startlingly than at that moment of danger. He dismounted every trooper and ordered their horses tied to the trees in our rear. Then he strung out our thin line as far as possible, so that the enemy's line would not overlap us, and we marched boldly up to the opening and began a rapid fire with our rifles. By this front we completely deceived the enemy and held him to his first line until we were reinforced with a part of our army. With this our force was increased to about half the number facing us, and General Forrest now felt that he must force the fighting in order to defeat the cavalry before the Union infantry could come up. Meantime, General Sturgis was urging his infantry through the intense heat. As the foot troops arrived almost exhausted, the Union cavalry was being pressed back, and Forrest's artillery and Bell's Brigade were swinging into view to reinforce the Confederates.

Forrest then resolved to stake the day on a charge against the enemy's infantry before it could gain time to rest and while their cavalry was falling back.

We were then instructed to take advantage of the thick undergrowth and conceal our advance as much as possible until very close to the enemy and then rush the line with our six-shooters.

Forrest announced that he would take one end of our line and Rucker the other, and that we could not fail. We believed it, because he had never failed. Dismounting and drawing their pistols, Forrest and Rucker placed themselves in the line of battle and went forward with us. As we moved, there was not a word spoken in the throng—only a tense and anxious hurrying, as much as was possible in such a thicket. As we advanced, we were searching with anxious eyes every turn and undulation of the landscape to discover the enemy's line, when suddenly the long, massed column, only a few feet in front of us, rose from a prostrate position to their knees and delivered in our faces one of the most withering rifle fires that our men had ever encountered. We were almost close enough to be powder-burned by the blaze from their long Springfield rifles, and the fire staggered us into a momentary confusion; but Forrest was there, and a single blast of his clarion voice was worth five thousand men in that vortex of danger and doubt. We were fighting an enemy that had two to our one, and nothing but our confidence that, in some way, Forrest would lead us to victory, could have sustained us. His escort moved as one man with him, and, with revolvers drawn, we charged the line of infantry before they could reload. Every man in our line had from five to ten shots, and we made them count. They broke in confusion and got away pellmell, but not before we had riddled them unmercifully. I never saw in any battle of the war as many arms and legs amputated as were lost at the field hospital at Brice's Cross-Roads. It seemed that every pistol ball found its human mark. If it did not kill, it pierced an arm or a leg.

When the Union commander brought up his brigade of negro troops which had been held in reserve, he told the blacks to form in line and allow the defeated white troops to pass to their rear, and that they would reform and support them; but about the time this arrangement was made, Barteau's regiment, which had been sent around to fall upon the rear of the Union column, made its appearance, and out artillery began to rake the retreating white troops with grape and canister. The brigade of blacks took to their heels without firing a shot and scattered through the woods like wild deer.

After the war, I knew an old negro in Corinth who was in the battle of Brice's Cross-Roads, and I asked him one day if he ran away from the battlefield. He replied: "No, boss, I didn't run; I flew."

A cold appraisement of this fight shows it to have been one of the most remarkable of all military history. With a force but little more than half as large as his enemy, this strangely gifted fighter of the Confederacy shattered a trained army of 8,000 men, and chased the remnant back to its base, forcing it to a speed seldom equaled in the wildest panics of war. The panoplied and militant host of Sturgis consumed nine days in the march from Memphis to Brice's Cross-Roads, but, with Forrest on its trail, what was left of that host covered the same distance on the return in two nights and one day.

We captured 250 wagons and ambulances, eighteen pieces of artillery, 5,000 stands of small arms, 500,000 rounds of small-arms ammunition, and all the enemy's baggage and military stores.

But, notwithstanding the great victory, this battle took heavy toll from our ranks.

> "Like the leaves of the forest when summer is green,
> That host with its banners at sunset was seen.
> Like the leaves of the forest when autumn hath blown,
> That host on the morrow lay scattered and strewn."

CHAPTER 20

HARRISBURG AND
TUPELO, MISS.

THE next raid into our territory was commanded by Gen. A.J. Smith, a West Point soldier.

The department commander at Memphis had collected another special army to overthrow Forrest and his troopers and to gain control of the only territory then entirely open to the armies of the Confederacy.

In view of the many disastrous attempts to crush Forrest, the Union officials collected a large force of all arms and gave the command to a general who was expected to take no chances of defeat. About the first of July, 1864, this army moved out from the vicinity of Memphis, proceeding with great caution over the main highway so recently traveled by the army of Sturgis.

Forrest was acquainted with the man with whom he had to deal, and advised with his superiors as to the safest plan of defense.

My understanding at the time was that Gen. Stephen D. Lee had been sent by the authorities at Richmond to support Forrest, with all available troops that could be spared from the other theaters of the war.

As General Lee was the senior and ranking officer, of course he was in command of the Confederate forces; and while he evidently desired General Forrest to act with all possible freedom, yet, however generous the superior commander, the question of military ethics necessarily made for both commanders a delicate and sensitive situation, which could not but hamper the judgment and the action of General Forrest, for, thus subordinated, his was not the supreme responsibility.

Of course, I, a mere boy, had no touch with the source of official information as to these grave matters, except through chance expressions of those higher up, as to what had been discussed in the councils of war.

At any rate, while the Union column was approaching New Albany on the Tallahatchie River, it was freely discussed that General Forrest desired to distribute his force among the hills just south of the Tallahatchie at New Albany and strike the Union Army on its flank while marching. The theory was that, thus surprised, the enemy could be beaten in detail, as it would be impossible to mass his attack.

It was by such tactics that Forrest had thus far defeated every force he had met, and I personally believe that if he could have had his way we would have routed this force as we had all others.

On the other hand, it seems that Gen. S.D. Lee thought it best to bring up all possible infantry and artillery which could be secured from Mobile and Vicksburg and mass it for a decisive battle in the vicinity of Pontotoc, Miss., forcing the Union Army to fight us on ground of our own choosing or to make a retreating fight and abandon the expedition.

No doubt this plan would have worked admirably but for the fact that General Smith discovered the trap and refused to walk into it. After threatening Pontotoc, he suddenly turned to the left and moved toward Tupelo, being well on the way to that place before we were aware of his intentions.

On the morning of the 13th of July, Forrest began the chase, and we soon came up with the rear and captured some wagons and a cannon before the enemy could turn back and fight. Having only two regiments of our command, we could only annoy the enemy, as he was trying to reach the railroad by nightfall. Upon reaching the hamlet of Harrisburg, some two miles west of Tupelo, the Union Army threw up some temporary breastworks in the edge of an old field or clearing and prepared for a defense. In my opinion, this was the most unfortunate fight in which the command of General Forrest ever engaged. We lost more men and were more severely repulsed than in any other fight.

After a terrible battle, lasting all day, both sides were willing to quit. The Union Army was satisfied that they could go no further south, and on the morning of the 15th commenced a retreat toward Memphis, Forrest nagging their rear at every step.

They turned on us at Ellistown, Miss., and we had a sharp fight. Here General Forrest was wounded in the foot and had to give up the chase personally. The Union Army returned to Memphis, defeated in its plan to destroy Forrest and his command and to invade the all-important grain fields of the Confederacy.

CHAPTER 21

RAID INTO MEMPHIS

EEPLY disappointed over the many futile and disastrous attempts to vanquish Forrest and his troopers, the Union Army headquarters again, about the month of August, 1864, assembled a formidable army and marched it into Mississippi, fully determined to crush this bold Cavalier of the South. General Forrest was fully informed as to the numerical strength of his enemy, and he knew that he was so outnumbered that his only chance was to win by his wits. Indeed, this necessity was not new to him, but it had never been so great as at that time. With a handful of men and a legion of original and brilliant ideas, this untaught genius had piled up a list of victories which will never cease to be the wonder of the military student.

In that latest crisis and danger to our little army and to our cause we, who had so long followed Forrest, knew not what strategic plan was being worked out in his brain; but we were one in the thought that he would find some way to save the situation. How unique and almost unbelievable was his plan!

When the advance of the blue army had been pushed to Oxford, Miss., Forrest instructed General Chalmers, one of his division commanders, to gather all of the force that was left and put it in battle array before the enemy, and to parry the advance as much as possible without bringing on a decisive engagement. By these tactics the Union commander was deceived into looking for and preparing for a pitched battle each day.

While the situation rested thus in the balance of expectancy, Forrest selected from each unit of our army a squad of picked men, well mounted and equipped. Placing himself at the head of this special troop, without a word of explanation, he bade us follow him; and, with hearty obedience and blind confidence, we obeyed, grimly ready for whatever desperate enterprise awaited us at our unknown destination. We headed toward the west, crossing the Tallahatchie River, and then turned northward in the direction of Senatobia, Miss., and the Cold Water River. All bridges and crossings of these rivers and their tributaries had been rendered impassable, and we were forced to all manner of inventions to get over the streams. At one place we made a pontoon bridge, with grapevines as the main support, and carried the floor planks from a barn a half mile distant.

At daylight on the morning of August 21 we rode into the suburbs of the city of Memphis, Tenn. It was as if we had come down out of the sky on winged horses, so great was the surprise to Generals Washburn and Hurlbut; and these commanders, by a margin of two minutes, escaped from their headquarters in night attire, leaving uniforms and paraphernalia of every kind. The boldness of the stroke saved us. There were enough Union troops in Memphis to have surrounded and captured us, but they fled to shelter, and we had possession of the town for three or four hours. We captured several cannon and a number of prisoners, but the swiftness of our mission made it necessary that we leave all of these behind.

In leaving the city we fought everything that made the slightest show of resistance, but there was no organized effort to interfere with us.

When we reached the city limits, General Forrest returned General Washburn's uniform and other clothing taken from his headquarters in the early dawn, and some time afterwards General Washburn had a new Confederate uniform made and sent to General Forrest.

This expedition had the desired effect. The headquarters knew not what designs lay behind the strange and startling raid into the very heart of the military government of that department, and the army of invasion was hurriedly recalled to protect Memphis.

Thus again had the untutored Forrest, with the strategy of a Hannibal or a Frederick, substituted his wits for guns and soldiers and chased an army with his genius.

We wended our way back to Mississippi and to our command, men and horses weary, worn, sleepy, hungry, and tired, but with the happy consciousness that we had vanquished the foe from the gates of Oxford without the loss of a man.

> "Up the broad valley, fast and far,
>   The troubled enemy had sped.
> Up rose the glorious morning star,
>   And the mighty host had fled."

CHAPTER 22

RAID INTO NORTH ALABAMA
AND MIDDLE TENNESSEE

I N a short while after the Memphis raid our commander decided to go east and break the line that was furnishing Sherman's supplies while on his advance into Georgia and the Carolinas.

About the first of September, 1864, we marched easy to the Tennessee River, crossing at Florence and Bainbridge, Ala.; and after several small fights and skirmished, we appeared before Athens, Ala.; on September 16, 1864. At this place the Union Army had a strong Garrison, defended by a fort and blockhouses. The latter defense was impregnable to the assaults of infantry and cavalry, but as easy mark for artillery.

When we approached this stronghold, rain was falling, and I was put forward on the skirmish line just before daylight. We marched only a short distance before we drew the fire of the enemy. Nothing was visible except the quick flashes of flame from the guns on either side. We were instructed to lie down and hold our position until daylight. After a few rounds, both sides decided to cease firing.

As the light began to dawn, our line advanced and drove the enemy inside his fortifications.

After a quick survey of the situation, General Forrest decided that it would be best to try to "bluff" the Union commander. Accordingly, he was notified that Forrest's full command was at his gates, able and ready to overwhelm him, and that he could avert a useless sacrifice of life by an immediate surrender. The plan worked, and the fort proper was surrendered, and the men walked out and became prisoners.

In the west side of the town was a large blockhouse, with a full regiment as a garrison. The commanding officer refused to surrender, and in response to the demand he sent a defiant message, challenging the Confederates to come and take the place. This officer thought the attackers were only cavalry raiders, without artillery; but his enlightenment was not long delayed. General Forrest ordered Captain Morton to bring two guns into action. We placed the guns in a street overlooking the fortification. The first shot barely touched the top of the fort, and the second shot tore straight through the center. Before the gunners could reload, a white flag was run up. We had possession of the town and all its defenders.

While the details of the surrender were being arranged, we heard a train coming in from the direction of Decatur. General Forrest hurriedly sent Lyon's regiment to fall in behind the train on its arrival and block its return. It had brought a regiment of Union soldiers to reinforce the garrison. They jumped from the flat cars and lined up behind a row of cordwood along the railroad. The train hurriedly backed out and made its escape. We were lined up on our horses, and the enemy began a very harassing fire, which had a telling effect on men and horses. Colonel Kelly, our commander, ordered us to dismount and charge the foe from his position behind the cordwood. Meanwhile, General Lyon was advancing upon the enemy's rear, with his skirmishers well in front. The retreat of the Union column from our arrack was so rapid that it ran over Lyon's skirmish line and captured it. This skirmish line was in command of my boyhood friend, Capt. Henry C. Klyce. Further on in these memoirs I shall refer to him again. We had this new regiment at the mercy of a simultaneous front and rear attack, and its position was hopeless. Captain Klyce, their prisoner, told the commander that we had them surrounded; that we had captured all the troops in the town, and further resistance was useless. Captain Klyce protested against the injustice of thus uselessly subjecting the Confederate prisoners to the fire of their own men; but the Union commander stated that he would not surrender while his men were being fired upon, and that he was unwilling to require one of his men to go forward to announce the desire to surrender. Then Captain Klyce volunteered to go forward and make the announcement in the face of a brisk musketry fire. He carried a white shirt on the point of a bayonet; and, of course, our firing ceased as soon as he was seen, but not until he had faced the gravest danger for the sake of friends and foes. In the midst of the brutalities of war it is such unselfish and heroic acts as this that sublimate the spirit of battle.

CHAPTER 23

———

SULPHUR TRESTLE, ALA.

———

The capture of the Union Army at Athens, Ala., was indeed the fulfillment of a great necessity with us. We took over a large supply of provisions and camp equipment, twenty carloads of clothing, a number of horses, several cannon, and about 4,000 small arms, with a quantity of ammunition for same.

On the day following the fall of Athens we moved against Sulphur Trestle, in Alabama. At this place the railroad had spanned a small stream with a high, covered bridge, which was of such consequence to the Union Army that a strong fort and garrison were maintained here, guarded with mounted cannon. When General Forrest examined the structure, he was satisfied that we would have to fight for it. The commander promptly refused to comply with our demand for a surrender.

There were good positions for our batteries, but the gunners would be dangerously exposed to the fire of the sharpshooters of the fort, and the only way to protect them was to march an attacking force across an open field to a point within range of the fort, so that we could direct a continuous fire against their loopholes.

The crossing of that field and the bloody results made an impression upon me that time cannot efface. In all the fights I had engaged in up to that time I had never had an uncomfortable foreboding of danger, but in that strangely charged hour I had a presentiment that I would not get through; and as we rode toward the place where we were to dismount for the charge, I confided my feeling to my companion and asked him if he would be willing to exchange places with me in case it should fall to his lot instead of mine to hold horses. (It was the plan of our commander that every fourth man in the line should hold horses in the rear, while the others were charging as infantry.) He promised; but when the show-down came, he flickered; and I went forward as usual, for I had never acted as a horse holder. The enemy's artillery was firing at us incessantly; and as we turned the top of a slight ridge, Colonel Kelly's horse was killed and fell just a few feet behind my position. As we cleared the hill and came into full view of the fort, we were met with a veritable hail of lead and iron. We were charging in a run, but men were falling at every step. We moved close up and lay down and kept up a continuous fire until our batteries reduced the fort and caused it to surrender.

Just as we reached the stopping point I was in the act of firing, when a ball struck my left hand between the first and second knuckles. It passed entirely through my hand and struck the trigger guard, knocking the gun violently against my head, and I thought for the moment that I had been struck by a cannon ball. I was practically unconscious for a few moments; and when my senses returned, I was lying on the ground, very sick, my head roaring like a freight train, and the wound in my hand bleeding profusely. Our battle line was flattened out on the ground within fifty yards of the fort. Quite a number in my immediate location had been wounded, and one poor fellow within a few feet of me was moaning pitifully, when a bullet struck him in the center of the forehead and killed him instantly. When I saw this, I told the boys that as I could not fight, I was going out of the danger zone. They thought the risk of making the run in full view would be greater than to remain in the line; but I did not like the idea of lying there helpless in a veritable slaughter pen, so I took the chance, and evidently outran the bullets, as I got back through that awful open field without being hit. Just as I thought I was out of danger, I heard a shell coming, as it seemed, on a bee line for me. To dodge it I flattened myself on the ground; and as I looked up, I saw that the shell was fully a hundred feet above the ground. It exploded about a half mile from where I lay. I think that was the last shot from the fort, as it was surrendered in a few minutes. I chanced to meet Col. D.C. Kelly, our commander, and he gave me a drink of water and bandaged my wound with a napkin.

I then went to the field hospital, where the surgeon dressed my wound and gave me something to quiet my nerves. When night came, I slept; and in the morning that followed I learned that a number of my comrades had gone away on the long and silent march beyond the gates of eternity.

After being wounded, I was sent south with other disabled soldiers. We had also about 5,000 prisoners captured at Athens and Sulphur Trestle. I rode my own horse to Cherokee, Ala., where the wounded were separated from the prisoners and guards.

At Cherokee we were given a temporary train of cars, in which the wounded were transported to Okolona, Miss.

On this trip, by the merest chance, I met a former slave of my father acting as porter on our train. He was a practical barber and a general handy man. His interest in me was intensified when he saw my condition, and he took the tenderest care of me until I was able to leave.

After the war was over and this former slave and I were both citizens of Corinth again, with earnings of my own I bought him a good barber's outfit and set him up in business.

It is a regrettable fact that the world, with its garbled histories and its false legends of violence, will never understand the true relation between the master and the slave of the old South.

That there were many individual cases of brutality, there can be no doubt, and that slavery as an institution of human government is wrong, no right-thinking man can deny; but in all the records of mankind there is nothing that parallels the conditions and practices which governed that slavery, now forever banished from the industries of our beloved country and expunged from its Constitution.

The gentleness and sympathy of the masters of Dixie and the faithfulness and loyalty of the black slaves should be jealously written into an impartial history of that South that was but is no more. They are the incontrovertible evidences of the greatness of our people who inherited the dark burden of human bondage from another age and who were innocent heirs to the sunny lands of cotton and cane, on which alone, of all our wide country, this shackled, tropical race could labor with profit to their owners.

During those awful years when every Southern home was the probable stage of a tragedy it was not uncommon to see only the mistress of a plantation left with her children in the care of her slaves, who stood by her and respected and protected her through every danger.

After the army left Sulphur Trestle, General Forrest gave his attention to the destruction of forts and blockhouses up and down the Memphis and Charleston and the Louisville and Nashville Railroads. While thus engaged, we threatened Pulaski, Tenn., sufficiently to hold a large Union force there behind breastworks, so that they did not attempt to interfere with our raids.

To hold the Union garrison at Huntsville, Ala., on the Memphis and Charleston, within its works, we threatened it with the division of General Buford.

The one unfortunate feature of our continued successes was that we could not save and put to use the vast amount of stores captured on these raids, in view of the sore need of them among all the armies of the Confederacy.

Our mission was to hit as the lightning strikes—to wreck and terrify and then disappear.

Our enemy had no cavalry force in this theater of the war that could cope with us, and his slow-moving infantry and artillery found us a moving target, too swift and restless for their sluggish aim.

CHAPTER 24

———

FOURTH INVASION OF
WEST TENNESSEE

———

S oon after the close of the Middle Tennessee raids we began our fourth invasion of West Tennessee, which section had already yielded to us so bountifully of the sinews of war in men and equipment.

The Union commanders were yet unable to solve the mystery of Forrest's ability to descend unseen upon their strongholds and escape unhurt with all the spoils of war and leaving destruction in his tracks. Their shrewdest tacticians had failed to trap him, and their overwhelming armies could not crush him.

About the 12th of October, 1864, our command pushed out toward the Cumberland and Tennessee Rivers; and on October 29, near Johnsonville, Tenn., we captured the transport Mazeppa, loaded to the guard with all kinds of military supplies. The boat was one of the richest prizes that had ever fallen into our hands. We towed her to the bank and unloaded everything our commander would permit us to take out, and then set fire to the boat and destroyed her, with the bulk of her valuable freight.

General Forrest told us to each take a new outfit of clothing and blankets and enough food for three or four days, and not to add another ounce, as we would have to fight like the devil to get out of there.

Among other things, I took a pair of fine cavalry boots. Securing the tops together, I swung them across my saddle and filled them with parched coffee, then a very rare luxury in the paralyzed markets of our stricken people.

On October 30, 1864, we captured four more transports with cargoes similar to that of the Mazeppa; and although the armies of the Confederacy and the civilians of the South were in the straits of poverty, we could do nothing but destroy these rich stores.

On November 4 we appeared before Johnsonville, Tenn., where there was a fort and a large depot of supplies. In an effort to cut off the enemy's fleet of gunboats on the river just above Johnsonville we captured two of the dreaded monsters and destroyed them.

After getting our field guns into position opposite Johnsonville, we opened fire at daylight on the boats and the large warehouse. The boats hustled away as rapidly as possible, but not until we had sunk some of them and crippled others.

The fort opened on us with two big guns, making a might noise, but doing no damage.

Our batteries soon set fire to the warehouse and the wharf, and destroyed all supplies within reach of our guns.

General Sherman, commenting on this raid, said that it was a feat of arms that won his highest admiration. With a cavalry force and a few field pieces of artillery, General Forrest had captured and sunk several gunboats and transports on a navigable river and under the protection of a fort.

The grand result of this expedition, covering about two weeks, was the capture and destruction of more than $7,000,000 worth of property, with a loss of only six men killed and perhaps a dozen wounded.

After the lapse of nearly sixty years, in contemplating the career of this untaught Hannibal of the Southern Confederacy, we find that the three tallest peaks of his fame are the pursuit and capture of A.D. Streight and his raiders, the battle of Brice's Cross-Roads, and the Johnsonville raid.

These three exploits will forever hold aloft the name of Nathan Bedford Forrest.

CHAPTER 25

THE BEGINNING OF
DARK DAYS

RETURNING from the Johnsonville raid, we met the army of General Hood. We were ordered to take the advance, and on November 19, 1864, our command was assembled at Florence, Ala., on the north bank of the Tennessee River, at the foot of the great "Mussel Shoals." General Forrest was placed in command of all the cavalry, and we began the advance on Nashville. During this march I suffered some of the severest hardships of my life.

Gen. George H. Thomas, one of the ablest of the Union commanders, had collected a large force of all arms, and was confronting Hood at every turn of the route. We, in advance, came in contact with his cavalry a number of times, and I had many thrilling and narrow escapes. General Wilson, of the Union Army, had a well-equipped cavalry force of 10,000 men, and Forrest had to contend with this force with about half its number.

We kept the Union column moving backward day by day until we reached Spring Hill, Tenn. Here we came in contact with Slocum's Corps; and after a severe fight, we pushed them back into the town, and had that column of the enemy separated from their main force, which had retreated on Franklin, Tenn., a short distance beyond.

Here a great mistake was made by someone other than General Forrest. It is not my purpose to criticize, but I shall state facts and let the reader judge for himself.

At Spring Hill night came on soon after or about the time the battle closed, and Forrest moved his command around parallel to the pike that connected Spring Hill and Franklin.

Hood's main army came up after nightfall.

Thomas had pushed on to Franklin, leaving Slocum and Wilson to hold the Confederates in check at Spring Hill until night, when they were to withdraw under cover of darkness.

I have no personal knowledge of what took place on that night between our commanders, but it was current talk, and had been published many times since the war, that General Forrest sent a message to General Hood urging that either our command or an infantry division be ordered to take position across the Franklin and

Spring Hill Pike to prevent the uniting of the two Union columns. That this was not done was a blunder that laid the foundation for disaster to Hood's army.

While I do not know what passed on that fateful night in the high councils of our leaders, I do know that, as Forrest's command lay through the long, uneasy night along that pike, we plainly heard the artillery and wagons of the enemy's army marching out of Spring Hill and away from sure defeat and capture, which would have been their fate had they kept their position until daylight of another day.

The next day General Hood arrayed his army in battle order under the expectancy that the enemy would make a stand at Franklin.

After the lucky escape from Spring Hill, our foe utilized to the fullest possible extent every natural advantage in preparing for a defense at Franklin. Earthworks were hurriedly thrown up, and every house and fence was intelligently utilized to retard the momentum of an open attack.

The soldier who undertakes to tell what he actually sees of a battle as extensive and terrible and bloody as was the battle of Franklin has but little to tell, and so I shall attempt no description; but that dreadful conflict of November 30, 1864, is known to every student of history as one of the great disasters of the Confederacy. There were a greater number of Confederate officers killed at Franklin than at Shiloh, Chickamauga, or Gettysburg, to say nothing of the bloody and one-sided slaughter of our men.

I never shall forget the gloom that settled over the ranks of our beaten troops. The blunder at Spring Hill seemed to smite the hearts of our men as they contemplated its deadly cost; and yet that great mass of men, with embittered souls, prepared to press onward.

The night following the battle the Union Army withdrew to Nashville and entrenched for the expected assault.

Though vastly outnumbered, Hood moved at once and invested the city of Nashville.

From the 2d to the 15th of December we held the enemy within his fortifications. On the 15th he moved out and tried in vain to break our line. On the 16th he renewed the sortie with increased masses of troops, and our left wing collapsed and forced Hood to retreat. And what a retreat! No one who participated in it can ever forget the suffering and hopeless anguish of that weary, running march.

The cause for which this grand army had so nobly fought, tottering toward its every battle-field, was now living only by the gameness of its defenders.

Defeated and shattered amid the desolation of winter, hungry, half-naked, and footsore, this suffering host turned sadly from the capital city of one of its own loyal States, and followed its haggard gaze toward the deeper South, with the benumbed feeling that somewhere, somehow it would make another stand, if only to give the last impulse of its fast-ebbing energies to the spirit of its dying cause and perish with its hopes.

General Forrest was ordered to cover the retreat, and the brigade of General Walthall's Mississippians was assigned as his infantry support.

Knowing our sad plight, flushed with victory, and eager for the finish, the Union Army started in pursuit with 10,000 well-mounted and well-equipped cavalry under General Wilson.

Forrest had about 5,000 cavalry, and Walthall's men numbered about 2,800; but as they were almost destitute of shoes and clothing of every kind, we had to carry many of the men in the wagon train, using them only when we were forced to stop and fight.

Hood had planned to get to the Tennessee River, where we had a pontoon bridge, at Mussel Shoals.

With what consummate genius General Forrest kept the ravenous foe from the heels of that almost helpless host as it marched and stumbled and fell forward toward its goal of temporary safety, is a matter of record and need not be here set forth.

After many days of rear-guard fighting, in which the skill and daring of General Forrest parried and blocked and retarded the swiftness of our pursuers, we succeeded in holding the enemy in check until the gray remnant of Hood's once magnificent army crossed the Tennessee at Bainbridge, Ala. The pontoon bridge was quickly destroyed, and the Union Army, foiled in further pursuit, turned down the river to Eastport, to which place boats brought supplies and troops.

Here General Wilson prepared to match against Selma, Ala., then the "heart of the Confederacy."

CHAPTER 26

THE LAST FLICKERING
OF THE GREAT FLAME

ANUARY, 1865, found General Forrest bending every energy to the maintenance and recruiting of his force for whatever further defense might have to be made, and the Union commander at Eastport making careful and extensive preparation for an extended and determined campaign as soon as the weather conditions should be favorable.

It was with great difficulty that we managed to feed ourselves and our horses through those trying months of bleak winter.

In the ranks, where men had never shirked a duty or a danger, the sad story of our lost cause was already forewritten in our suffering hearts; and the hopelessness of our situation became so fixed in the soldiers' minds that desertions became frequent; and in order to check this and enforce discipline, our commander resorted to stern measures, to the extent that some of the deserters were executed and their bodies conspicuously displayed as a warning.

While crossing the bridge at Tuscaloosa, Ala., I witnessed one of these tragic and morbid spectacles, which made a lasting impression upon my youthful mind and embittered my heart against all wars.

Late in March the Union Army began to move southward from Eastport, and General Forrest's first interest was to ascertain the enemy's plans as far as possible.

I was with a scouting troop when we luckily intercepted and captured a Union courier carrying the plan of the Union commander's line of march. This message was sent to each of the division commanders.

They were ordered to move into South Alabama in three columns, marching parallel to each other, twenty miles apart, and to consolidate at a point north of Selma, Ala.

We speedily sent this information to General Forrest, then in the vicinity of Tuscaloosa, Ala.

General Wilson had 10,000 or 12,000 veteran troops of all arms, while Forrest had about 5,000, and only half of that number were of his veterans; but we had the advantage of being on our native heath, and our leader had never been beaten in a single case when he was in supreme command of all dispositions and details of the battle.

With their plans in hand, he sent General Chalmers to meet the extreme eastern division and General Jackson to take the middle division, while he would personally direct the movement against the western column, nearest Tuscaloosa, in the hope of defeating it and then falling upon the rear of the main column.

But this was not to be. When Forrest was ready for the move, he sent a courier to the Selma garrison and to Roddy's cavalry, with full information of the whole plan; but the enemy captured the courier, and General Wilson changed his plan, and Forrest never knew why until after the war.

While our forces, ignorant of the change of plan, were separately waiting for the three columns, we ran into Wilson's cavalry, 8,000 strong, at Bogless Creek, a few miles north of Selma, and we had only about 200 men, mainly the escort.

Forrest, thinking that we had run into a small force, threw us hurriedly into line and charged the advance, and the enemy thought they had struck the main Confederate column. We soon got into a mix-up, and they began to overlap us in every direction. The bulk of our little band was fighting and falling back in an effort to clear a passage, when we discovered that the enemy was making a move to cut General Forrest off from his troops. About ten of us went to his assistance. They had him surrounded, and he was fighting like a lion at bay. He killed several men—no one ever knew how many; and when he came out of the circle, he jumped his horse straight through a cordon of mounted men and escaped without a mark on his person.

We fled the field and fell back to Selma, Ala.

Here the Confederacy had been operating a small manufacturing plant for making arms, and the commander had only enough men to make a thin picket line for the protection of the plant.

When Forrest arrived, he gathered every available man and put them in the trenches for the best possible defense.

Forrest's plan having failed, he was in ignorance as to where his troops were, and this gave the enemy a very dangerous advantage.

Forrest felt that if the enemy had slipped by his commanders they would follow him up and strike him in the rear when the attack on Selma should begin.

At any rate, it was certain that when the Union Army should reach Selma there would be a fight of some kind, regardless of odds.

The escort took position in the trenches on the extreme left, the weakest point, and Roddy's troops were placed on our right. Then the home guards and mixed multitude were strung out in a thin line along the remainder of the works and instructed to hold the trenches at all hazards and never leave until they should receive orders to retire.

Of course Forrest told us that if we could hold the enemy in check for a while, our missing troops would strike him in the rear soon, and that we could capture or destroy the cavalry force; but, unfortunately, Forrest was not on the outside with his troops, and the capture of our messenger had so shifted the situation that the commanders of Forrest's two columns lost touch, and never knew anything about the battle until it was all over.

On the first approach to our line the enemy seemed to have about 2,000 men, and we held them in check and pushed them back out of range; but on the second charge they came like the locusts of Pharaoh, and that thin line of gray did not tarry for the impact, but went, self-ordered.

Forrest held the escort company until the enemy had swarmed all around us and cut us off from the city by way of the bridge. He then mounted his horse and told us to follow him—that he was going out. It looked like a desperate undertaking, but we had dared Fate so many times and "gotten by" that we believed that our great captain would carry us out again.

Our company was formed into a flying wedge, and began the drive toward the southwest, so as to strike the river at its narrowest point.

We fought like demons, as the majority of us in that company had never surrendered, and we did not now intend to do so.

I had many narrow escapes. My hat was either shot off or carried away by a saber stroke, but I got through without a scratch. When we cleared the cordon that had surrounded us, we plunged our horses into the river and escaped by swimming to the opposite shore.

Here Forrest gathered the few of us that were left, and we made our way out in the direction of Gainesville, Ala. We had lost a number of the escort in the fight—some were killed, some were drowned in the river, and some were wounded and surrendered. Among the captured were my two brothers and a young man who afterwards became my brother-in-law, R.P. Elgin.

After we were safely on the way to Gainesville, I told General Forrest that it seemed to me that the war was over, and that I was going to my father's house. He and family were then refugeeing in the flatwoods of Pontotoc County. With but few words, the General admitted the gravity of the situation, and told me to go on to my father.

I first stopped at Okolona, Miss., where I was treated with great deference and kindness by the same slave boy who had nursed me when I was wounded.

From Okolona I went to my father and remained until June, 1865.

From Pontotoc County I rode back to Corinth, secured employment, sold my horse for $150 in greenbacks, and started my first savings account, from which I afterwards started a business of my own.

On my return to Corinth, I had found the town garrisoned by a troop of negro soldiers.

The whole prospect was a picture of desolation, as this town and vicinity had been under the very heel of war for four long, weary years; but nature had not forsaken the landscape entirely, for it was carpeted with grass and clover and wild flowers—a beautiful winding sheet for the dead hopes and prospects of the buoyant boys who had marched away from this place under the Southern battle flag.

There were practically no domestic animals to trespass on the fields and meadows; but while the husbandman had forsaken his gardens and vineyards to kill his own kind, the unmolested birds and wild animals native to this clime had restored God's original paradise and were living in happy groups and families upon the lands which ungrateful man had deserted.

Three years after my return from the war I was married to Miss Juliette Elgin, of Huntsville, Ala., a beautiful and petite young lady of 118 pounds. She is with me yet; and whatever changes time may have wrought upon her appearance to other eyes, with the eyes of memory I behold her still, and the mental and spiritual graces of her youth have only ripened with the years.

To this union were born two daughters, Luella and Lucille, to increase our responsibilities and brighten our home. To train and educate them became the prime purpose of our lives, and in their welfare and happiness we submerged our personal ambitions.

Now that they have homes and family responsibilities of their own, our fireside had lost them; but in their happiness we find our recompense, and this humble record of sacred memories is affectionately dedicated to their sons.

In drawing to a close this record of memories, I trust that I may be pardoned for a brief indulgence of recollections which cannot be of interest to any save my own people and, perchance, my comrades of the sixties.

I was born at Jacinto, in the pine-embowered hills of Tishomingo County, Miss., and a good portion of my war service was happily given to guarding that sacred land which had nourished my joyous childhood.

With the tear-dimmed vision of retrospection, I ever behold that happy spot—its orchards, its meadows, its wildflowers and sparkling waters. Especially do I stand again with expectant thirst at the cold spout spring that gushed from the hill—eternal wonder of nature that sings on to the centuries to mock the fleeting vanity of our short lives. The trees and vines that shadowed my rest or my play or refreshed me with their luscious fruits can never fade. The fragrance of the wild grape's high-hanging bloom comes to me across the vanished years, and, with it, the flavor of the muscadine wrapped within its leathery skin. And as I dwell upon these fragments of youth's vanished paradise, I hear again the sad, sweet song of Tishomingo's pines—the same that sang to the Chickasaw Indians before the white man came.

That county, which was the world of my young and impressionable life, seemed to me to hold all that was necessary to human happiness. Its territory was equal to the State of Rhode Island, and three rivers were born within its borders—the Tombigbee, the Hatchie, and the Tuscumbia. Even to my unsophisticated mind there was something in the grandeur and the freedom of the place that spoke of things beyond the senses of the body. Like all the Indian countries, it had its mysterious landmarks and its sad and beautiful legends of the wars and loves and tragedies of the wild, savage, brave people whose crude road to God was through the "happy hunting ground."

My boyish imagination deeply colored with the glory and the romance of those vague traditions, I have stood, in the shadow of moonlit nights, and watched the dark heads of the pines nodding to the sky, and thought that, perchance, their whispered song was the echoed sigh of the vanquished red man brooding, in spirit, above the land he has so loved.

Another scene that flutters through my memory like a fantastic dream is the darkening forest of the evening twilight hour, alive with uncounted thousands of wild pigeons, turning the silent woods into a Babel of musical chatter as they gathered to rest in their sylvan lodge.

These all have flown away on the wings of time, as utterly as the great herds of the buffalo have vanished from the plains of the West, and, so far as I know, not a single bird of this species is left in our country.

For some strange reason the God of nature has permitted spoiled man to waste the myriad wonders of the virgin woods, until only the rivers, the springs, and the eternal sky are left of the glory that was.

In melancholy recollection of all the people and all the things beloved that are gone from that small, though great, green country of my early life, I salute thee, O Tishomingo of sacred memories!

This reverie may be meaningless to the majority of my readers; but it this, my heart's humble tribute to the remembered beauty of my native land shall meet the eye of a single companion of those blissful days and enchanting scenes, he will understand and the others will forgive.

CHAPTER 27

———

RECONSTRUCTION

———

Much has been said and written of that unhappy period immediately following the Civil War—unhappy for both the North and the South, because its memories delayed the reunion of our sections through many years. The humiliation and griefs of that frightful era left far deeper scars than did all the sabers and swords and bullets from Bull Run to Appomattox. The flame of war had burned out the lives of thousands of our brave sons and consumed our homes and wasted our lands, but the embers of reconstruction seared their mark upon the very souls of our people.

We who know do not charge that horror to the great nation to which we are as loyal and true as any beneath the flag to-day, but to individuals who abused authority and misrepresented the spirit of the North toward the South.

I, for one, thank God that our people themselves settled the problem of reconstruction by the application of a righteous courage to a desperate situation, but there was one influence in that settlement which was never generally appreciated. Across the closed chasm, above the graves of all the soldier dead, the great men of the North and the great men of the South looked at each other in silence and understood when the oppressors were driven from the South.

As soon as the insidious tongues of a few intermeddling, ignorant, vicious men and women, seeking to be the ministering angels of the former slaves, were hushed by the stern policy of the representative Southern people, the happy and natural relations of the two races were restored; and to-day, after nearly sixty years of freedom, the black man of the South knows that the Southern white man is his truest friend, because he alone understands him and sympathizes with his natural and legitimate needs.

As one who in a very humble way helped to make that sad history, as the representative of a family who owned slaves, I desire to here record my opinion that in the trying period following the war it was the Christian fortitude of our people that saved the day for us. Out of the ashes of material wealth, out of anguish and humiliation, we came with honor; and the unbroken spirit of the old South, serene amid its earthly poverty, is the unquestioned and priceless heritage of our sons.

Whenever and wherever I meet a soldier of the sixties, no matter whether he wore the blue or the gray, I think of his life as the figure and symbol of a sad, eventful day. His youth represents the morning, and it was filled with golden dreams. Achievement and success smiled before him, and his heart leaped with love, just as young hearts leap to-day. But, before he could realize his dreams, a great storm—that awful war—came and swept away his fairest prospects. The noontide of his life found him busy with the wreckage of the morning, and then it was that there rose in his soul a far greater courage than that which had sustained him on the bloodiest battle field—the courage to meet and conquer adversity, the divine grace to cast away his bitterness and to love his former foes.

My comrades, out of the ruined morning and the rebuilding toil of the noontide we have come at last to the evening and the twilight. Time has placed upon our heads his crown of silver and of snow. For us the long day of life is near spent, and the world can never chide us if, in the spirit of fraternity and forgiveness, we find ourselves dreaming backward toward the blood-billowed years of Shiloh and Chickamauga and all our other fields of mutual and glorious memories.

All of us who are now living in the true spirit of liberty and union know that out of our great war of sixty years ago has come a greater peace than our nation could have ever known had we not cut away, with the sword, the great mistake of the fathers of our country.

Let us pray that our sacrifices, now far back in the years, may be truly recorded, to be the living evidences of American courage—that tried and true courage which is our greatest asset, an asset of national wealth outweighing the value even of our vast material wealth.

Embodied in our sons and grandsons, only a little while ago, the whole world glimpsed that the same spirit of courage and patriotism on the battle fields of Europe, when the "Blue and the Gray" turned to "Olive Drab" and our boys, millions strong, crossed the ocean to defend the ideals of our country—ideals of national life which are rapidly becoming the ideals of all truly civilized peoples of the earth.

I rejoice that I have lived to see the greatness of America dawn upon the world. I rejoice that when the hour struck for the flag of universal liberty to "go over the top," it was carried there by the substance of our fields, by the power that came from our mountains of coal and iron, by the whirring wings of our liberty motors, and by the unbeaten and unbeatable soldiers of the United States.

For one hundred and forty-seven years the individuality of the American soldier has defied the analysis of military critics and upset the theories of every nation that had met him on the battle field.

Since his first far-off shot of Lexington, the makers of war maps have been unable to chart his power from his visible numbers, for in his unconquerable spirit there is the might of unseen legions and the unmeasured force of just and democratic purpose, as an armed host, is bivouacked in his soul.

You may follow his history from his advent into the world of political contention, through his almost unbelievable and unbroken line of successes, and you will find him, always and everywhere, the one unbeatable force which cannot be weighed in the scales that determine the military values of all other peoples. If other evidences were lacking to establish these facts, certain incidents of the World War alone would prove them. In no case did he fail to meet the test of fire; and the anxious world stood aghast when the German staff reduced the question of fighting ability to an absolute test in the hope of proving the weakness of our "raw recruits" when pitted against soldiers not only trained, but bred and born, in the iron atmosphere of the "Great Empire." The Germans, confident of their superiority, man for man, felt that such a test would weaken the morale of the American soldier and boost the waning German hope at Berlin.

On April 20, 1918, at Seicheprey, in the Toul Sector, a picked German column, the product of a century of militarism, assaulted an American force approximately equal numbers.

Not only was it a clash of men; it was the deadly embrace of principles—the death grapple of human systems.

The world knows the result. The individuality of the American soldier was asserted before the astonished eyes of all nations, and the Stars and Stripes floated triumphantly over that field of death.

Unafraid of all the military camps of the earth, this strange civil soldier, while fostering and guarding the greatest of all republics, has eschewed the damning principles of militarism, ever preferring to keep his sword sheathed in the peaceful scabbard of industry, drawing it only when Liberty is endangered.

Of that deadly way, which, directly or indirectly, involved every square inch of the earth's surface and the fate of every human being, living and yet to live, Hendrick Van Loon has beautifully said:

"The human race was given its finest chance to become truly civilized when it took courage to question all things, and made 'knowledge and understanding' the foundation upon which to create a more reasonable and sensible society of human beings. The great war was the 'growing pain' of this new world."

CHAPTER 28

———

AMERICANISM TRIUMPHANT

———

THAT Americanism which to-day is a dominant world force is not alone of North or South or East or West. Out of the blended greatness of all the sections of the United States came the hope of peace and universal democracy in that dark hour when the allied armies of Europe were backing doggedly toward the tottering gates of Paris. That hope was born of the reunited blood of the gray and the blue armies.

As it was Americanism that tipped the doubtful scale of victory on the field of battle, so it was Americanism that inspired the war-sick world to seek the great League.

And now that all eyes are turned toward Geneva as the chosen capital of the earth, the fascinating history of that far corner of Switzerland will be lifted by a thousand pens from the dust of neglect. Poured into the stream of current literature, it will add mellowness and flavor, as if a flagon of old wine were resurrected from some long-deserted cellar and poured into the spiritless punch bowl of to-day.

This new seat of world deliberation had ever been a home of thought—a place of dreams.

From the brain of a dreamer who dreamed there more than a hundred years ago there issued a ghost—the most monstrous and terrifying that ever looked from the pages of fantastic literature—for a century considered only a gloomy fancy of a wonderful imagination, but now revealed in the light of the world revolution as a hideous prophecy of the terror and agony of the great war. Perchance the prophecy was an accident. It may be that there was nothing miraculous—no inspired vision back of the dream; and still it may be that some yet undiscovered force of mind and soul mirrored in the brain of that bright dreamer the troubled future of the world and caused its expression in the mental creation of a monster.

In reviewing this ghost of accidental or miraculous prophecy, as the case may be, it is well to remember that this country of landmarks and memories has ever held a charm for the restless spirits of genius. The hill of Geneva is cathedral-crowned. Its unique and historic river, born of snow and ice and reborn of a crystal lake, divides the city like a stream of blue and trembling light, and the lands that sustain its countryside are a succession of orchards, gardens, and vineyards.

The beautiful Lake of Geneva, touching the city with its western extremity, stretches eastward for more than forty miles. Great spirits of many centuries have gathered about this place of dreams to sing their songs to all the future or work out their messages to mankind—poets, philosophers, painters, sculptors, theologians, astronomers, and scientists.

There Calvin lived and taught and died. There Rousseau was born to be the siren of free thought, and from that base of dreams went forth to lead his life of wonderful, dissolute, and brilliant vagabondage.

And so the list of the great whose live have touched this charmed and charming place could be extended on and on; but let us leave this to the research of the interested, while we pass to the immortals who are linked with our strange story.

In the eventful summer of 1816, while all Europe was being adjusted to the new sensation of living without fear of the great Napoleon, then just settled in his cage at St. Helena; when Germany, at last free from his dominating genius, was already beginning to steel the national heart for a career of supermilitarism, there came to the lonesome shore of this famous lake Lord Byron, the poet Shelley, and Mary Godwin (afterwards Mary Shelley).

Mutually possessed with the spirit of mysticism which seemed ever to brood over the moss-grown city, the beautiful lake and its environs, these impressionable children of nature entered into a playful contest to determine who could write the most harrowing story dealing with the supernatural. At least, it is known that Lord Byron, Mary Godwin, and Bryon's physician entered the contest. So supremely terrifying was the story of Mary Godwin that Byron never finished his story, and the story of the physician is unknown to the world of literature.

Her story tells of the secret ambition and dreadful realization of a German student of science in the University of Ingolstadt. Pushing his clandestine research into the realm of the unknown until he discovered the secret of human life, ambition kindled in his soul to mimic the master work of God. He created a soulless body of a man, and, by the application of his discovered chemical, infused into the cold, dead form the vital spark. It did not step from his touch as Adam stepped from the Divine Hand—in beauty and in grace—but came groveling into consciousness, a distorted monster. The student fled from his work; but in the silent hours of the night that followed, his horrid creature stood, with bloodshot eyes, above his bed, and, with hideous face and wildly waving arms, cursed the daring intelligence which had called it from the night of nothingness into an unnatural and miserable existence. Again the student fled, and continued to flee from the awful work of his hands; but ever the monster followed, penetrating the barriers of his most secret lodgings, begging death at the hands of its creator, or silently pressing against the pane of his window a face of suffering and rage. It murdered his friends and the members of his family. It pursued him through life, and at last stood and shrieked above his coffin—a terrible witness to the folly of his wisdom. Its work of vengeance ended, it stepped into a self-kindled fire and perished.

Could it not have been that this monster was more than a fantastic dream of Mary Godwin's brain? Did not this imaginary German student, misusing the discoveries of science to ape the power of God, foreshadow the mighty German nation harnessing every art and discovery of civilization for the creation of a monster a thousand times more terrible than that of the strange story—the monster of Militarism? Have we not seen this German-created monster, with body of steel and breath of fire, go forth to terrorize the world? Failing in its unnatural purpose, have we not seen it, like the awful ghost, turn upon its creator and hound a dynasty to its death? And is not this monster, like the other, now perishing in its self-builded fires?

Beautiful Mary Shelley! You cannot arise from your long sleep to answer our anxious question and tell us whether your uncommon story was the picture of a dream or the record of a vision!

Ring on, the soft bells of your golden past, O Geneva, and keep the sweet cadence of their ancient song to mellow the newness of your greater life to come! The heart of the world will beat within your gates; and may truth and liberty, clear and changeless as the waters of your Rhone, flow from the deliberations of your gathered wisdom.

EPILOGUE

———

THOMAS Dudley Duncan (1846–1931) lived only nine years following the publication of his *Recollections*. He had enjoyed a full life by the time his memoir was published in 1922. Following the War, he settled in Corinth, Mississippi, and employed himself in many capacities. Among them at various times were merchant, clerk, postmaster, weigh master for the inspection bureau, and inspector for the Mobile and Ohio Railroad. It was in his retirement years when he penned his *Recollections*. He devoted his time to his family, who were prominent Corinthians.

The father of two daughters, Duncan was a family man. Luella Duncan was born in 1868 and married Shelby Hammond Curlee. At times, the couple resided in Corinth and St. Louis, Missouri. Shelby Curlee was a successful clothing manufacturer, instrumental in both the Corinth

Clothing Manufacturing Company and Corinth Woolen Mills in Corinth and Curlee Clothing Company in St. Louis. Curlee was one of the highest paid executives in St. Louis in the late 1930s. He owned a substantial estate overlooking the Missouri River. Eventually, Curlee and his family purchased the historic Veranda House (later known as the Curlee House), built in Corinth in 1857. It used as a headquarters by officers from both armies during the American Civil War, among them Confederate Generals Braxton Bragg and Earl Van Dorn and Union General Henry Halleck. Prior to his death, Shelby Hammond Curlee created an endowment for the old Corinth City Cemetery, a gift that has greatly enhanced its preservation. Luella (Duncan) Curlee died in St. Louis on October 27, 1936. Her husband passed on January 31, 1944. They were buried in the old Corinth City Cemetery.

Duncan's second daughter, Lucille Duncan, was born on December 4, 1878. She married William Peyton Dobbins, a one-time superintendent of the local public schools. Their son, William Peyton Dobbins Jr., one of the grandsons to whom Duncan dedicated his book, became an attorney in the San Antonio, Texas, area before dying in 1980. A widow by 1930, Lucille resided in Middlesex County, Massachusetts. She was living in San Antonio by 1932 and remained there until her death on October 11, 1952. She was buried in Sunset Memorial Park in San Antonio, many miles and a lifetime away from her sister and parents in Corinth, Mississippi.

Juliette (Elgin) Duncan died on June 4, 1925, and was laid to rest in Henry Cemetery. Duncan himself lived another six years and died at the advanced age of eighty-five on September 19, 1931. He joined his wife in Henry Cemetery, his legacy slowly enshrouded in the mists of time and history. We are fortunate that Duncan chose to record his memories of the war that shaped and defined both him and the Nation.

Following Duncan's death, little attention was paid him in succeeding decades. His life largely faded into the mist and fog of distant history. His little book of recollections was largely forgotten and seldom referenced. Despite seemingly having been proverbially everywhere during the war, Duncan was not one of the memoirists regularly celebrated or discussed. His memoir appears to have been published only once, in 1922, by McQuiddy Printing Company in Nashville, Tennessee. Exactly how many copies were printed is not known, but the book was and is not plentiful. Perhaps a new chapter may be added to the epilogue of Duncan's life with the publication of this edition of Duncan's

Recollections of Thomas D. Duncan, a Confederate Soldier.

INDEX

Illustrations are indicated in *italic* type.

Index

Y

Z

www.ingramcontent.com/pod-product-compliance
Lightning Source LLC
Chambersburg PA
CBHW032056080426
42733CB00006B/294